SPEAKING TRUTH

Speaking

TRUTH

Women RAISING
THEIR VOICES *in* PRAYER

J. PAIGE BOYER, EMILY PECK-MCCLAIN,
SHANNON SULLIVAN, THERESA S. THAMES, JEN TYLER

Foreword by BISHOP VASHTI MCKENZIE

ABINGDON PRESS
NASHVILLE

SPEAKING TRUTH
WOMEN RAISING THEIR VOICES IN PRAYER

Copyright © 2020 by Abingdon Press

All rights reserved.

Library of Congress Control Number: 2019953510
ISBN 13: 978-1-5018-9834-1

Scripture quotations unless noted otherwise are taken from the Common English Bible. Copyright © 2011 by the Common English Bible. All rights reserved. Used by permission. www.CommonEnglishBible.com.

Scripture quotation noted IB is taken from The Inclusive Bible: The First Egalitarian Translation, copyright © 2007 by Priests for Equality of the Quixote Center.

Scripture quotation marked MSG is taken from THE MESSAGE, copyright © 1993, 1994, 1995, 1996, 2000, 2001, 2002 by Eugene H. Peterson. Used by permission of NavPress. All rights reserved. Represented by Tyndale House Publishers, Inc.

Scripture quotations marked (NIV) are taken from the Holy Bible, New International Version®, NIV®. Copyright © 1973, 1978, 1984, 2011 by Biblica, Inc.™ Used by permission of Zondervan. All rights reserved worldwide. www.zondervan.com The "NIV" and "New International Version" are trademarks registered in the United States Patent and Trademark Office by Biblica, Inc.™

Scripture marked NKJV is taken from the New King James Version®. Copyright © 1982 by Thomas Nelson. Used by permission. All rights reserved.

Scripture marked NRSV is taken from the New Revised Standard Version Bible, copyright © 1989 National Council of the Churches of Christ in the United States of America. Used by permission. All rights reserved worldwide. http://nrsvbibles.org/

20 21 22 23 24 25 26 27 28 29 30—10 9 8 7 6 5 4 3 2 1
MANUFACTURED IN THE UNITED STATES OF AMERICA

For all the women who have spoken truth to power. May your voices be louder than the injustices of our world.

Contents

FACING LOSS

TRANSFORMING CRITICISM

LIVING GRATITUDE

Foreword

*"On the Sabbath we went outside the city gate to the river, where
we expected to find a place of prayer. We sat down and began to
speak to the women who had gathered there."*

Acts 16:13 NIV

"When the women gather, great things happen."

Leymah Gbowee
2011 Nobel Peace Prize

Women: we're innovators, detail tenders, and strategists. We're thought leaders, trendsetters, and change agents. We're entrepreneurs, educators, and domestic engineers. We're colleagues, collaborators, and clergy. We're corporate executives, visionaries, artists, and scientists. We work our nine-to-five and come home to work some more. We've made bricks without straw, lemonade without lemons, and a home without a living wage.

Too many women live in a cultural landscape that makes them believe that they are less than who God says they are, which is certifiably fearfully and wonderfully made (Psalm 139). We have righteousness, sanctification, wisdom, and redemption (1 Corinthians 1:30). We are already blessed with every spiritual blessing. We are heirs, chosen, holy, blameless before God and made complete in Christ. We are a children of the Most High God, accepted by Jesus Christ (Romans 15:7).

We've suffered in silence because of the insurmountable challenges that create for us a life that doesn't ever quit. But not anymore.

Women are speaking up and taking a stand. They are raising their voices in government, judicial systems, school houses, college campuses, and at vigils and demonstrations on issues that matter to them. Women have been gathering for generations to birth human service agencies, institutions, justice, social care platforms, and worship.

A Chinese proverb states, "When sleeping women wake, mountains move." Jesus says, "The simple truth is that if you had a mere kernel of faith, a poppy seed, say, you would tell this mountain, 'Move!' and it would move. There is nothing you wouldn't be able to tackle" (Matthew 17:20 MSG).

Speaking truth is where potent prophetic women begin to gather. In the Bible, Miriam gathered the women to sing a praise song after the miraculous crossing of the Red Sea. Lydia and other women gathered to pray outside the city gates of Philippi at a place Paul expected to find a place of prayer. He sat down to speak to the women who had gathered there. Lydia received the gospel and her house became a new church plant.

These handlers of the Holy are gathering us together in prayer group to pray prayers that move our mountains—from finding voice, facing loss, cultivating peace, transforming criticism, and cultivating a life of gratitude. The prayers become a focal point of our own prayer life. They plant seeds of conviction and confidence. They reflect that the Lord has given these prayer warriors the ability to take what life has handed to them and transform it into something greater.

Speaking truth is praying past disappointment until hope arrives. It is birthed by heavy burdens that have highjacked our peace. Prayer instigated by disappointment shows us how to pray until our mountains move.

Awake, dormant queen! There are mountains to move. Shake the stars from the tresses of your hair. Remember whose you are and adjust your crown. Rise above the messaging that undermines our radiance, resilience, and relationship with Christ—not that your race be won, queen, but that God's will be done. Selah!

Vashti Murphy McKenzie
Presiding Bishop
African Methodist Episcopal Church
10th Episcopal District
Dallas, Texas

Introduction

Women are powerful and pissed; women are also fierce and fed-up. Women have been joining hands for the purposes of societal change for decades. Women of faith have been guided by the Holy Spirit to work together to bring down injustices, even when they are perpetrated by women, and to build on the foundation Christ laid for the beloved community of God on earth.

This book is women joining together, yet again, because they are ready to speak up, speak truth to power, and act in new ways in response to the increasing challenges of our day. This book offers to all women the sustenance we need if we are going to do what we are called to do in the face of blatant racism, bigotry, sexism, heterosexism, and xenophobia out in the world and in the church. We greet these challenges knowing that the Good News of Jesus Christ is bigger than any societal ill and knowing God has called us to play a part in God's work of transformation.

We are indeed tired, but this is not a book about exhaustion. This book gives testimony to the power of God and the power of women to work and be energized by the God who creates us "for such a time as this" (Esther 4:14). This book acknowledges that life is hard and that we can't just "positive-think" nor "self-help" our way out of all the difficulty.

When we pray together and act together, we claim a new vision for how things can be—a vision God gives us through Scripture. We can support both ourselves and other women as we learn to find and claim our voices and end the silences imposed upon us. We can lean on one another for support when we face loss, recognizing that we aren't alone and don't need to suck it up and move on. Even though we can't control the storms of life around us, we can cultivate peace within our own hearts, in sisterhood and community. We can hear criticism launched at us, disregard what is not helpful, and transform the rest. We can practice living gratefully, even if only for the small things. When we are in the mire of sexism, racism, failure, infertility, loss of relationships or jobs, we can rely on our faith to help us change our lives and even the world around us. When things get real, we speak truth.

Finding Voice

Former Secretary of State Madeline Albright once said, "It took me quite a long time to develop a voice and now that I have it, I am not going to be silent."[1] This is *our* truth: women are *not* called to be silent, but to claim our voices and to speak our truths.

Women are silenced throughout Scripture, reflecting the way we have been treated throughout the millennia. Noah's wife was not even given a name, much less a part in the covenant with God (Genesis 9). Tamar spoke out against her rapist, only to be told, "Keep quiet about it for now, sister; he's your brother. Don't let it bother you" (2 Samuel 13:20).

Women have been misplaced, undervalued, underappreciated, and silenced. In the wake of #metoo and an increasing number of glass ceilings being shattered, we are witnesses to women claiming our presence and voices in powerful new ways. The very faith we proclaim, with Jesus as our resurrected Savior, *demands* we use our voices to speak truth with confidence.

Too often, women have been silenced by the world around us. Today we stand together. We refuse to be silenced; we refuse to passively watch the world pass us by. As women, we are finding our voices and raising them like the women did that first Resurrection day: though men (and others) around us have not been quick to listen or believe, we, like Mary, speak truth anyway (Luke 24:11). We lead anyway.

When we pray, act, and speak together, we claim a new vision for how things can be: a vision that honors women before us like Ruth, Tamar, Mary, and the countless women who remain unnamed, both in Scripture and in our modern world. That is what you will find in the pages of this section: we are raising our voices and telling our stories as women of faith.

Jen Tyler

*"Come and see a man who has told me everything I've done!
Could this man be the Christ?" They left the city and were on
their way to see Jesus. Many Samaritans in that city believed in
Jesus because of the woman's word when she testified, "He told me
everything I've ever done." So when the Samaritans came to Jesus,
they asked him to stay with them, and he stayed there two days.*

—John 4:29-30, 39-40

The story of the woman at the well is one of my favorites in scripture. It's a Samaritan woman's conversation with Jesus, where she realizes he is a prophet, but rather than ask for miracles or blessings, she speaks on behalf of her people. She is one of the first social activists we see, and she is holding Jesus to account for the actions of his people.

I identify with this woman and her willingness to take advantage of a random circumstance and hold power accountable. As a transgender woman, the question of the power of my voice is one that I have faced on many occasions. I have spoken to power and expected that the power would be dismissive. All too often, the expectation was met. I left those conversations feeling I had wasted my breath; dejected, frustrated. I have also been quiet when I should probably have spoken up, because I had no wish to be dismissed again. I believed that my voice lacked the power it should have had.

Yet this outcast woman spoke from the margins, and then, emboldened by having met Jesus and heard his words of acknowledgment and encouragement, she left. She then gives a simple message in her town, but that message leads to the moment of evangelism. She isn't just Martha complaining about how much Mary is helping in the kitchen; she leads her entire town, a culture used to the margins, to see Jesus. Verse 39 specifically gives credit to her for the belief of many in the town. Her testimony brought them to a new, more inclusive existence.

I think of that when I think of her. I think of the impact her persistence had in dealing with authority, and the impact her story had on bringing belief. I wonder if she knew the power of her voice before that moment. Those times I would rather be silent, how much more would my voice help bring change? Those times I think I need stronger, more prophetic words, why don't I realize how prophetic my simple story already is?

Today, I have found my voice and begun to grow it. Scripture tells us that the power of our voice is in the words given to it, not from the power within. And this scripture tells me that a woman simply speaking her story and standing up to power can bring change.

Prayer: Genderful God, I am forever grateful for the voice you have given me and the strength you have given to it. Help me learn when and how to use it so that your work might be accomplished and your love better shown upon this world. Amen.

Caroline Anne Morrison

*Then the LORD stretched out his hand, touched my mouth, and
said to me, "I'm putting my words in your mouth. This very day
I appoint you over nations and empires, to dig up and pull down,
to destroy and demolish, to build and plant."*

—*Jeremiah 1:9-10*

One evening when I was in third grade, my teacher called my parents.
My stomach hit the floor and my heart started racing. My mind was
reeling with what I could have done wrong. Tears welled up in my eyes and
were streaming down my face by the time my mom got off the phone. It
turned out, I was too quiet in class. Through my sobs, I explained that I
was afraid I would get in trouble if I talked, and I had been placed at the
table of rowdy kids in an attempt to calm them down. It didn't work; it
only increased my fear and my silence. I was afraid my voice would betray
me and get me in trouble. Then, a decade later, after wrestling with my
faith due to the immense injustice I saw at an HIV/AIDS orphanage in
Thailand, God called me into pastoral ministry.

My call is to build others up, to tear down the patterns of this world
that keep sick eight-year-old boys in orphanages and poverty, and to destroy the church's apathy toward the hurting and abandoned. With this as
my message, I also knew my voice would get me in trouble. However, the
Lord called me and promised to put the words in my mouth, just like God
did for the prophet Jeremiah.

The very first time I preached, an older gentleman came up to me and
told me I would settle down one day and "get over my passion." Nearly
ten years later, it hasn't happened. My voice gets me in trouble regularly
now—just ask my church. And while my fear rises up trying to silence
me like I was nine years old again, the power of my calling rises higher.
Perhaps trouble is the place to be when speaking the truth is what put you
there.

We are each given a message to proclaim wherever we are. Often that message isn't one people want to hear and will likely get us in trouble. As a result, we have two choices: to let fear silence us or to speak up and speak out. When we speak God's words, we can have confidence that while some things may be destroyed—like relationships or governing structures—God is already building up to something new, something better, something to give all a place to worship and know our Savior.

Prayer: God who speaks in chaos and in silence, strengthen my voice. Strengthen the voices of all those you have called and to whom you have entrusted your message. Even when fear swells, tune our ears to the sound of your calling. Amen.

Stephanie Rupert

*Thou didst not despise women, but didst always help them and
show them great compassion. Thou didst find more faith and no
less love in them than in men.*[2]

—*Teresa of Avila*

I think what I felt was a sense of enlightening and awe when I learned
that all the medieval female mystics were ambitious in the way that they
revealed themselves as "female mystics" or "female prophets" in a world
of patriarchy of the Dark Ages. There was no way for women to become
"somebody" in the Middle Ages, and God was the only way for women
to claim their voices. In a world haunted by extreme gender inequality,
female mystics found a way of self-actualization through their own unique
spiritual conversion experience. By their spiritual experiences and intimate
union with God, female mystics were able to achieve a position of leadership and make an impact in the world. They actively sought to fully
self-actuate themselves within the cultural framework where women's becoming or even being was basically denied.

Teresa of Avila, my favorite female mystic, was a sixteenth-century
Carmelite nun and reformer, declared a Doctor of the Church over four
centuries after her death.[3] I especially love the story of Teresa traveling
to one of her convents when she was knocked off her donkey and fell
into the mud. She got up, dusting off her rear end, and said, "Lord, you
couldn't have picked a worse time for this to happen. Why would you
let this happen?" And the response in prayer that she heard was, "That is
how I treat my friends." And Teresa said, "And that is why you have so
few of them!"[4]

I love this episode because of her sense of humor and audacity in talking
back to God. At the moment I read it, I instantly fell in love with Teresa
of Avila. I was in my early twenties and desperate to find the meaning of
my life and calling in a world where still it is hard to claim it as a young
woman. Through Teresa, God says, "I do not despise women, but always

help them and show them great compassion. I find more faith and no less love in them than in men."

Prayer: God, let me be audacious in this world where it is hard to find my voice and place. In union with you, I can find my identity and calling. Amen.

Hyewon Sophia Hyon

⌒ A Prayer for Being Seen *and* Heard ⌒

God, history has recorded the silencing of women like me, from the beginning of time until now. Pop culture and mainstream media have objectified my body and cheapened the value that is my very existence. Even the current leader of the free world has made clear his belief that my sisters and I are subject to the groping of a man's hands and words . . . in silence. God, even now, I recall the lessons of my childhood that were much more demanding than those taught to the boys. These lessons taught me, as a "young lady," that it was much more important for me to be concerned about "how" people would see me rather than "if" they would hear me.

Appearance over voice was always the mantra. Now, God, in answering your call to stand boldly and to speak against the injustice in this world, I often find myself struggling to be liberated from the expectation of silence, and I grow weary, even afraid. I want to be among those bold enough to lift my voice and say, "Enough!" . . . "Me too!" . . . "My life matters!" But when I open my mouth, I often choke, and what actually escapes is nothing more than a mere, unintelligible whisper as I wonder how my voice will "look," rarely giving thought to how its sound might be the clarion call that liberates another.

Lord, I KNOW that you have called me for a time such as this and that there is power in my ability to freely speak my truth in testimony of your power and presence in my life. So, God, my prayer is that today and every day you will grant me courage to move beyond the grace of being seen into the boldness of being heard. Help me, oh Lord, to find my voice and to use it to the glory of your name and for your Kingdom's sake. I pray this prayer by faith and in the strong name of Jesus, the Christ. Amen.

Shazetta Thompson-Hill

*On another Sabbath, Jesus entered a synagogue to teach. A man
was there whose right hand was withered. The legal experts and
the Pharisees were watching him closely to see if he would heal
on the Sabbath. They were looking for a reason to bring charges
against him.*

—*Luke 6:6-7*

I grew up in a home with domestic violence, the hard-to-report kind that was filled with verbal, emotional, psychological, and financial abuse. We took turns taking the brunt of my father's focus, a time when nothing we did or said was right. Meanwhile, we walked on eggshells trying to avoid conflict. In this story of the Pharisees and legal experts trying to bring Jesus up on charges while he teaches on the Sabbath, I remember my experiences. My gut reaction to this scene is fight, flight, or freeze: the space in which I lived for so long.

Jesus turns the focus to the man with the withered hand, someone I realize I do not know until this point in his life. What I know from Jesus's stories and the history of first-century Palestine is that persons living with disabilities were living on the margins of society. By no means am I comparing my experience of domestic violence to the experience of living with disabilities. I relate to this man's healing journey. I have lived with adrenal fatigue and depression. Caring professionals and a class on healthy relationships have given me tools to move past my initial reaction, or trigger, and engage with people and their stories to make more meaning of my own experience.

Jesus, in his brilliant nonviolent strategy, responds assertively. He empowers the man who has suffered lifelong marginalization to step forward and stretch out his hand, a pivotal moment in this man's healing hero's journey.

I, too, have reached a pivotal time in my healing hero's journey. I have been invited to stand up, step forward, and reach out my hand to serve as a community educator for Safe Journeys in Illinois. Safe Journeys is an agency that works to end domestic and sexual violence in our communities through prevention, crisis intervention, and social change. I have found new life and healing in this work where I must stand up, step forward, and reach out my hand every single day.

Prayer: Healing Mother, draw back the veil of evil, injustice, and violence. Just as Jesus found a way to teach the people living on the margins of their inherent worth and wholeness, reveal to us creative, nonviolent strategies to invite the people in our communities into healing spaces filled with empowering movements and words. Amen.

Melissa Engel

Don't let anyone look down on you because you are young.
Instead, set an example for the believers through your speech,
behavior, love, faith, and by being sexually pure. Until I arrive,
pay attention to public reading, preaching, and teaching. Don't
neglect the spiritual gift in you that was given through prophecy
when the elders laid hands on you. Practice these things, and
live by them so that your progress will be visible to all. Focus on
working on your own development and on what you teach. If you
do this, you will save yourself and those who hear you.

—*1 Timothy 4:12-16*

It was the third time I'd been reamed out in public after a lifetime of being bullied. This was the beginning of my career, yet facing the reality of adult bullies was slowly destroying me. I no longer felt joy, hope, or motivation.

But this time, when I retreated to cry, I heard the voice of God saying, "You don't deserve this. You are my beloved." With a divine strength, I returned to the woman who bullied me. I calmly said that how she'd talked to me was not ok; as followers of Christ, we are commanded to speak to one another in love. She did not back down, but I did not escalate or re-engage. I simply stood my ground as a beloved child of God, worthy of respect and love.

In that moment, I began a journey back to myself. I could see the negative effects of my silence and the power of my voice. I was not the only one affected by this toxic environment. While I'd been internalizing the message that I didn't measure up, so had many others. Others felt unable and unwilling to lead because they didn't want to be in a position to be attacked. When I stood up for myself, several people thanked me privately for what I'd done. By standing up for myself, I discovered the power my example set to guide others to freedom as well.

Later, in encountering a new bully, I realized I wasn't afraid and I wasn't anxious about being attacked. In finding my own voice, I found the courage to stand up for others in a public way. That witness to belovedness in the face of bullying continued to ripple out.

It turns out that my voice matters. Not just for me. But for all who hear it. Paul reminds Timothy, and me and you, that our example matters. "Don't let anyone look down on you. . . . Don't neglect the spiritual gift in you. . . . Practice these things, and live by them so that your progress will be visible to all. . . . If you do this, you will save yourself and those who hear you."

Prayer: Loving God, too often, I have heard the attacks of this world more clearly than your voice of love. I confess that I sometimes hide the gifts and voice you've given me. Grant me courage today to publicly claim my belovedness so that I and those who hear would know your radical love and freedom. Amen.

Jennifer Burns

*Then the prophet Miriam, Aaron's sister, took a tambourine in
her hand. All the women followed her playing tambourines and
dancing. Miriam sang the refrain back to them: "Sing to the
Lord, for an overflowing victory! Horse and rider he threw into
the sea!"*

—Exodus 15:20-21

Moses's sister, Miriam, has always intrigued me. I can picture her
so vividly as a small girl, crouching behind reeds beside the Nile,
watching over her baby brother. I can imagine her singing and dancing
with a tambourine in hand, helping lead her people to freedom. Scripture
calls Miriam a prophet—a powerful word for any follower of God, but especially for a woman. Miriam was one who heard the will of God and spoke
it to her people.

Part of Miriam's work as a prophet was as a song leader. Some of my earlier memories are of being led in music by women. We sang all the classics
in Sunday school, from the tale of Zacchaeus to the power of the B-I-B-L-E.
Later, I discovered pop music. Women sang to me the woes of falling in
love, the need to rise up and be strong, and the fun of sisterhood.

Music has the power to connect us. How often have you turned to a
song that described exactly the mood that you were in? From heartbreak to
rebellion, songs can define our lives. Musicians are idolized in our culture
because they help us connect with the poetry of what it means to be human.
Music is part of our rituals, our everyday lives, our most special moments.
Music reminds us that our feelings are not isolated and unique.

So why not use the power of music to our advantage? Why not be
prophets who sing the truth to one another?

As women, we want to lift one another up. We want to help each other
find our voices, our power, our gifts. We can sing to one another the songs
of life and love. We can teach each other songs of freedom, of calling, of
truth. When the women around us are weak and unsure, let's sing to them.

Let's sing to them the songs that were sung to us. It is our job to carry on Miriam's prophetic work. We must take up the chorus, each of us together, so that new women can join the song.

Prayer: Holy One, you have sung to me songs of love and worthiness. Help me believe them. When I am at my lowest, open my ears to hear your song that I am a beloved daughter. And help me find my voice, to let it be loud and strong or light and beautiful, that it may be heard by those who need to know that they, too, are beloved children. Amen.

Heather Dorr

⌒ A Prayer for Finding Voice ⌒

Giver of Breath and Voice, when I find myself unable to speak, when the world has robbed me of my breath and voice, fill me anew with your powerful Spirit of peace and liberation. As I face the daily reality that my voice and my very being are not valued or celebrated, help me breathe in your grace and strength with every beat of my heart.

Help me absorb the knowledge that the Hebrew word for discouragement means "short of breath." Loving Breath, help me remember that every time the evil and malice of this world discourage me or cause me to be short of breath, I can pause, breathe, and regain my breath in you.

Mighty Voice, who called the very existence of the cosmos into being, remind me that you speak through me as I answer the calls you have put on my heart and life. Great Encourager, grant me unending courage, audacious faith, and powerful actions to lift my voice for your ever-coming kin-dom[5] of peace and liberation. Help me in every breath to bring forth your justice and joy.

Santo Dios, ayúdame a saber que en ti siempre tengo ánimo y siempre tengo mi voz. Ayúdame a luchar para que tu voz sea levantada en cada persona y en cada parte de tu creación. En momentos cuando estoy desanimada, lléname del poder de tu Espíritu Santo y usa mi voz para proclamar que todos somos una familia en Dios.

In the name of Jesus, who steadies our breath and gives us voice, we pray and live. Amen.

Paula Cripps-Vallejo

*Are not two sparrows sold for a penny? Yet not one of them will
fall to the ground apart from your Father. And even the hairs of
your head are all counted. So do not be afraid; you are of more
value than many sparrows.*

—*Matthew 10:29-31 NRSV*

D o you think Nana would have loved me if she'd known I was gay?"
It was a strange time to ask my father that question. In part, because we needed to already be on our way to the funeral, but mostly because
I was asking it in the presence of my Nana, who was lying in front of us,
dead in her casket. This seemed to be the last possible moment. But I still
felt her spirit near.

I had good reasons for putting off the subject of my sexual orientation
for so long. It had been a bumpy road coming out to my parents and by
the time things had smoothed over, Nana (my maternal grandmother) was
already ailing. There was just never the right time to bring up the subject,
especially considering all of the things she had previously said about homosexuals (not that she had ever used that polite a word).

Whenever she asked about my dating life, I would change the subject,
because she was the kind of person who never changed her mind. But then,
after she'd died, I wondered if, given the chance, she would have changed
her mind for me.

So often, we conceal the whole of who we are, simply because we cannot risk rejection. These words from Matthew remind us that God already
knows us fully and loves us deeply. And if we can trust in that divine love
and in our own worth, then sometimes we can find the courage to speak our
truth. Sometimes, we can even learn to trust that others, who are also loved
by God, are capable of more than we imagined them to be.

My dad leaned over the casket and spoke into my Nana's ear. "Hey. Your
granddaughter's gay," he said. Then he stood up and said to me, "She says she
still loves you." And we laughed and we wept. And we said our goodbyes.

Prayer: God of second chances, help us remember the depth of your love for us. Grant us the courage to trust in your love, and share our truth with one another. Amen.

Lindsey Bell-Kerr

In the year of King Uzziah's death, I saw the Lord sitting on a high and exalted throne, the edges of his robe filling the temple. Winged creatures were stationed around him. Each had six wings: with two they veiled their faces, with two their feet, and with two they flew about. They shouted to each other, saying:

> *"Holy, holy, holy is the L*ORD *of heavenly forces!*
> *All the earth is filled with God's glory!"* . . .

Then one of the winged creatures flew to me, holding a glowing coal that he had taken from the altar with tongs. He touched my mouth and said. "See, this has touched your lips. Your guilt has departed, and your sin is removed."

Then I heard the Lord's voice saying, "Whom should I send, and who will go for us?"

I said, "I'm here; send me."

—Isaiah 6:1-3, 6-8

We stopped in the tiny town of Sahagun after walking for hours. We had been talking and talking about God, our world, our discernment. They were a Catholic couple from Idaho, walking to pray. I was walking to find myself again. God had been walking with me through all of the pain and hurt that brought me to the middle of the Camino de Santiago. I told a few people that I was a pastor, but I had lost my voice. This walk was a chance to regain some of the things I had lost.

Sahagun is the halfway point on the French way of the Camino. It is a marker. A shift happens here. You turn from moving away into arriving in your search for God. This couple was stopping overnight here. I was moving on. They asked me, "We heard you were a pastor. Would you bless us?" I had not been pastor for half the journey even though I know now that I couldn't help but live into my call. I hadn't offered any services besides just showing up. I nodded. Yes, I could do this. I could bless my fellow travelers.

We arrived at the center of town. We bowed our heads. I placed my hands on their heads. I prayed for guidance and safety. I prayed for wisdom. I prayed for mercy. When we looked up, there was a line of pilgrims waiting to be blessed. An hour later, I continued my walk, with my voice full. I knew who I was again.

Isaiah was already clergy before this moment with God. Isaiah had been praying, teaching, and preaching for years before his mouth was touched. The world shifted and changed and in that moment, God activated Isaiah's voice. At a crucial point in history, politics, and social change, Isaiah's lips burned. He knew what he had to do. In the initial words of the passage, "In the year of King Uzziah's death. . . ." we know that God will do something radical. The writer might as well have said, "In the year Trump was elected. . . ." or "In the year kids were placed in cages. . . ." or "In the year that climate changes were ignored again . . ." In this year, our voices are ignited and found. They are lit and burning.

Prayer: O God, may my voice rise from within. May I speak into the occasion when called upon in the midst of this climate. May my burning lips create words inspired by your blessing and your call. Amen.

Courtney McHill

Then {God} said, "Come no closer! Remove the sandals from
your feet, for the place on which you are standing is holy
ground."

—*Exodus 3:5 NRSV*

When I was young, I loved being barefoot. I loved to feel the grass between my toes, or the contrast between smooth carpet and cool tile. It didn't matter if I was at home, outside, or in church, I always kicked off my shoes so there was nothing between the soles of my feet and the ground beneath me. When I was in middle school my pastor scolded me. "Put your shoes on! You're in church!"

"God told Moses to take off his shoes," I quipped back.

"When God speaks to you directly, you let me know. Until then, keep your shoes on."

So I did.

As I grew older, I let those other voices tell me what I should and should not do. Wear this, don't wear that. Speak up, don't talk so much. Not that theology, this theology. Not those words, these words. Slowly the barrier between myself and the Ground of All-Being grew thicker and thicker. I lost my confidence, lost my spunk, lost the whisper in my soul that had first called me to stand on holy ground.

That changed when I attended a two-year academy through The Academy for Spiritual Formation, where I spent eight weeks in intentional community. While there I followed the rhythm of monastic life, sitting among scholars, pastors, and disciples. In silence and in worship I began to hear, once again, the still, small voice of God. Through sharing and leading worship I embraced my voice, finally realizing that my strong soprano did not have to be in competition with my call to pastor; it enhanced it. Through conversations and covenant groups, I was nurtured and affirmed: You are a mother. You are a pastor. You are a scholar. You are beloved. I walked barefoot through grassy fields, climbed trees, and buried a sparrow. A part of myself that had long been buried was resurrected.

Once again I am sure of what God has called me to do, which is going to mean some big changes in my life and vocation. But I'm ready now—ready to listen only to the voice of God, and not the nay-sayers. Ready to speak my truth whether my voice is strong or falters. I am ready to take off my shoes, to stand on the holy ground and do the holy work God has called me to.

Prayer: Holy God, give me courage to stand upon the holy ground you have called me to. Help me speak the truth you have placed in my heart, regardless of what others may say in response. Through it all, help me remain rooted in your never-ending love. Amen.

Amanda M. Rohrs

~ A Prayer for Agency and Power ~

Empowering God, you are the One in whom I live and breathe and have my being.[6] I know that I am your beloved child, gifted with a powerful call to be your person in the world. I know that I am powerful because of the seeds power you have planted inside of me. You unfold a path before me and invite me to be a cocreator with you as we journey together in love. Although I know all of this, I confess that I am tempted to doubt in my heart: I doubt my call, my gifts, my agency, my power. I often neglect to claim my agency or use my power because I am afraid. The familiar companions of anxiety and fear continually beg me to include them on the journey. Help me have the courage to remain firmly rooted in your love and power. Remind me of my identity and call. Give me the courage to claim and use power you give me to flourish and thrive in the places to which you have called me. Empower me to rise to meet the challenges of this day with confidence, power, and love. Amen.

Colleen Hallagan Preuninger

~ A Prayer for Empowering ~ Others to Speak

Almighty God, help me to listen fully and to commit my whole self to the needs of those whose voices have not yet been found, have not yet been heard. Guide me to be still, to open my ears, and to open my heart to hear the voice of one in need; to advocate for and encourage others to find their voices, and to help them find their courage to speak. Give voice to the voiceless, O God, and may I be a conduit for your strength and comfort, that they may know your Spirit is present, and your message is found in them. May your words be found in their voice, as I listen, rather than speak. Amen.

Jennifer Zeigler Medley

True belonging is the spiritual practice of believing in and belonging to yourself so deeply that you can share your most authentic self with the world and find sacredness in both being a part of something and standing alone in the wilderness. True belonging doesn't require you to change who you are; it requires you to be who you are.[7]

—*Brené Brown*

As a preacher, I lose my prophetic voice at least once or twice a year. I get weary in sharing a message from the Gospel that seems to fall on deaf or stubborn ears. There are times I feel that people are tired of hearing my voice and the message I bring. The comments start coming: "She used that word that we don't like," or, "We are tired of hearing sermons that make us uncomfortable. We come to church to feel good."

During times like these, I become tired and angry. I am tempted to stifle my voice or tame my preaching to be what others want to hear. But then the Spirit reminds me of my call to preach the gospel of Jesus, to share the good news, and to help people grow in their faith. I remember that while I am called to use my voice to comfort, I also use it to challenge, to proclaim, and to teach. At times the words are hard to hear. Voices are needed to name the injustices in the world that we are called to address as people of faith. To lose my voice is to lose a part of myself and the very message I am called to preach.

Our voices have much to do with our identity. People know our voices when they hear them. Children respond to them, even from within the womb. We use them to connect on deep levels with others. Our voices sing praises to God or are used to calm crying children or the sick and dying.

When we feel as if our voices are not being heard, are lost, or are drowned out, it often becomes difficult to find them again. When I am tempted to stifle my voice or hold back from using it in a prophetic way, I center myself in who I am as a woman, a mother, a preacher, a teacher, and a child of God. When I belong to myself and remember first and foremost that I belong to God, I am able to clear the voices in my head that bring me down or threaten to stifle my own voice. I remember that words hold the power to change the world, and I am emboldened to find my voice and proclaim the Gospel without fear.

How is God asking you to use your voice today? How will your faith be stronger than your fear?

Prayer: O God who gives voice to the voiceless, give me the strength to find and use my most authentic voice that I may bring glory to you in whatever ways that I am called to use it. Amen.

Jill Moffett Howard

{God} has told you, O mortal, what is good; and what does the
LORD require of you but to do justice, and to love kindness, and
to walk humbly with your God?

—*Micah 6:8 NRSV*

W hat if God wants us to be in the world with an overarching mindset of grace, rather than a legalistic finger-pointing way of life? What if God is trying to woo us into a new way of being in the world, rather than blindly doing what we've always done before? Micah 6:8 calls us to engage with the world, rather than step away from the world, and to embody a faithful life rather than "check off the boxes" of holiness.

Sometimes I find myself getting wrapped up in my own achievements. It is so easy to intertwine personal accomplishments—as worthy as they may be—with my own self-worth. And it is easy to come up with a list of goals to conquer in my personal and professional life. After all, our friends, our colleagues, and the media constantly remind us that there are always lists of goals we can reach for and celebrate as we achieve them.

It becomes exponentially more difficult to separate our achievements from our self-worth when our work, our service, and our volunteer energy are all connected to our faith formation. "But this work matters so much," we justify, knowing that we will be praised for our achievements, and that the work of our hands is in line with God's hopes for us.

Micah 6:8 is a clarion call for how we are to live in the world—we are called to "do justice, and to love kindness, and to walk humbly with [our] God." What if God's call for us in Micah 6:8 is not simply to take action in specific, one-size-fits-all ways, but a reminder that God longs for a way of being from us—a way of being in the world that is countercultural and much broader than simply following a prescribed set of rules? How would our faith expand and free us for joyful obedience?

Prayer: Gracious God, remind me that my self-worth comes from you, and not from my achievements. Reorient my life so that I live a life of justice and renewal, rather than reaching for earthly goals. Amen.

April Casperson

*Each person should test their own work and be happy with doing
a good job and not compare themselves with others. Each person
will have to carry their own load.*

—*Galatians 6:4-5*

For longer than I care to admit, I considered myself "bad" at public speaking. For many years, I have watched friends, family, and colleagues with awe of their eloquence. I would marvel at their beautifully worded prose and secretly judge myself for being too repetitive, or for stumbling over my words. After a while, I just accepted that I would always feel out of place speaking publicly.

To be honest, it wasn't just my fear of public speaking. I was constantly keeping track of what I felt like I was lacking as a leader. I had a list a mile long of things I "should do better." Over a retreat weekend, it hit me with full force that I had come to think of many of my own personality traits as a burden for me to manage and mitigate. I started to realize that my diligent work in trying to make myself look and sound more like others had instead made me lose track of myself and lose track of God. I was exhausted trying to hide myself, and I began to realize that I was not using the gifts, the voice that God had given me.

These words in Galatians are a much needed reminder for me. While my natural inclination might still be to compare myself to others, I am now trying to rediscover and appreciate who God has created me to be. Part of that work is to learn to speak the truth in love (Ephesians 4:15) to myself, to recalibrate my inner dialogue. To be able to be satisfied with my own work without comparison, embracing the imperfection.

It wasn't long after this retreat that I let down my guard a bit. As I spoke, I realized that I had forgotten that there were others there too. I realized that when I allow myself to let go of comparisons, I am freed to find the voice God has given me.

Prayer: Good and gracious God, thank you for the gifts you have given me. Help me discover more of who you have created me to be each day. Pour out your Holy Spirit upon me, and strengthen my voice and resolve so that I may glorify you; in the name of Jesus Christ, I pray. Amen.

Jessica Anne Richard

⌒ A Prayer for the Courage to Admit ⌒ What You Need

Compassionate God, I am always so busy worrying about everyone else that I seldom recognize what I need. When I finally see my own needs, naked before me, I am afraid. How dare I ask for what I need when I should be taking care of others? How dare I be vulnerable? It seems easier to swallow my voice and keep my head down.

"If I can just touch his clothes, I'll be healed," an unnamed woman thought as she approached you.[8] She had endured so much suffering. People around her kept telling her they knew what she needed. Physicians promised impossible cures, family members tired of her never getting better, and predators took advantage of her vulnerability.

Healing God, you know that I know how this woman felt . . . and you know how I relate to her. You know how my stomach is fluttering, how my brain searches for excuses. Too often, I fear admitting my own needs more than I fear enduring suffering. Give me the courage of that unnamed woman to reach out for what I need. Give me the confidence to name and advocate for what I need.

Amen.

Shannon E. Sullivan

Be on your guard; stand firm in the faith; be courageous; be strong. Do everything in love.

—*1 Corinthians 16:13-14 NIV*

Our world is increasingly polarized; you are supposed to pick a "right" side and stick to it. Yet as a follower of Jesus, I want to have boundary-breaking love like him, and so every time I see a divide, I am called to ask how I can love the person on the other side.

My current church is mirroring the deep polarization in our country, and as a result, is being torn apart at the seams. As a leader, I have realized how easy it is to befriend people whose theology and practices match my own and to build up a team of people who agree with me. For so long, I thought standing firm in my faith meant clinging to my beliefs, telling others they were wrong, and trying to change their minds so that their beliefs matched mine.

Recently, I befriended a colleague whose theology is different from mine. His background is more conservative, while mine is progressive. Our friendship started over beers and jokes, but as we've ridden the waves of our increasingly polarized world, our friendship has deepened. We've shared about the pain that exists in the deep divides in our world. We've cried over the brokenness around us. We've held hands and prayed.

I realized that standing firm in faith does not mean that I stand firm in what my faith looks like, barricading against others. Instead, standing firm in faith means rooting myself in love and asking how I can love others even, or maybe even especially, those I disagree with. It means pointing to injustice and oppression and naming it as evil but separating that from people. It means recognizing that each and every person is made in the image of God and we all need to be freed from racism, sexism, homophobia, able-ism, and all the systems that hold us all hostage. It's bringing our relationship to God in prayer and being open that God would transform both of us. It's a scary place to be.

I have realized that by rooting myself in love, I am invited to stand in a space of tension; a place where I can love people whose beliefs, faith, actions look very different from my own. Standing strong means that I don't need to give up what I believe, but it does mean I love them despite our differences. This is not easy, but it is where Christ calls me.

Prayer: Liberating God, transform my heart. Break down the walls that divide and free me from the bondage of oppression. Remind me that I am made in your image and invited to bear that image of love to the world. Amen.

Breanna Illéné

*There is a big difference, after all, between being silenced and
silencing oneself. And it is precisely because women like Teresa of
Avila and Julian of Norwich and Catherine of Siena knew how
to silence themselves before God that they gained such significant
influence over the Church in times when women had little voice.
In silence, I had found a reservoir of strength that, if I could just
learn to draw from it, could make my words weightier. In silence,
it seemed, I had finally found my voice.*[9]

—*Rachel Held Evans*

Like most women, I know the pain of being silenced. I've felt angry when a man repeatedly interrupted my presentation to re-explain what I just said. I've felt powerless when I was not taken seriously in my work because I "look like a teenager." I've felt discouraged when an institutional decision was made by a (nonrepresentative) majority vote that clearly put women at a disadvantage. I work in an organization where all people should be equally valued, but sadly, this is often not the case. I have experienced the hurt inflicted by patriarchal structures, sexism, and ageism. I know what it's like to feel voiceless, and therefore, powerless.

But I am never silenced by God, who has given me a voice and called me to use it. Instead, God invites me to silence myself so that I can remember who I am. Those who silence me are trying to force me to be who they want me to be; God invites me into silence to remind me who God has created me to be. When I stop talking, shut down my internal dialogue, and shut out all of the noise that seeks to interfere, I can hear God's voice and receive the power of the Holy Spirit. When I silence myself in God's presence, I receive the insight, conviction, and courage that I need to find and claim my voice.

The difficult thing is that silence is not easy to come by. I work full-time and have two kids; life is busy. There is a lot of noise in my life, literally and figuratively. It's challenging to find space and time to be silent, and even when I do, interruptions abound. But God's voice is not limited by circumstances of space and time. God is speaking and inviting me to silence myself to listen, however that is possible on a given day. I have heard God's voice just as powerfully while nursing a baby at three a.m. or exercising as I have on the pathway of a labyrinth or on a retreat.

Whatever form it takes, silencing myself in God's presence helps me remember who I am. It reorients me in relation to God and the world around me. For me, silence is the key to unlocking the calling and voice that is God's Spirit within me, urging me to speak truth with courage.

Prayer: God, I am grateful that you do not silence me. Help me silence myself in your presence, so I can hear your call to use the voice that you have given me. Grant me courage to speak truth as an instrument of your love, grace, and justice in the world. Amen.

Jessica Petersen

Do not remember the former things, or consider the things of old.
I am about to do a new thing; now it springs forth, do you not
perceive it? I will make a way in the wilderness and rivers in
the desert.

—Isaiah 43:18-19 NRSV

When a new opportunity, relationship, career, or project comes along, do you ever find yourself in a state of overthinking and self-doubt? Perhaps these feelings surface immediately, and you find yourself unable to take the first step. Maybe you begin confident, eager, and ready to take on the world, but when you hit an unexpected bump, the paralyzing fear sets in. No matter when the doubt, worry, or uncertainty strike—you are not alone!

The Divine is inviting us to be cocreators as we grow through life's experiences. While the Spirit is nudging us forward to witness and take part in the new thing, we hold ourselves back by focusing on the past. It might seem like you are trapped by negative thoughts or the haunting voices of others that can often make it difficult to fully explore and embrace a new opportunity. The call to not consider the former things is a difficult task because sometimes the past difficulties are all you can think about! It is the former things that are familiar and known, even if they are negative, and that can give us a sense of false comfort.

It takes courage not only to let go but also to walk away from the things in our past that do not give us life. Name the voices, either your own or those of others, and face them so that they no longer have power over you. God calls us to rise up from the ashes of what was and to courageously move forward to the new and unknown. We are invited to carry with us what we have learned, rather than being stuck in the pit of what was.

This new life often starts in the wilderness. In fact, the new thing that God is doing might even seem like a mirage! But look and reflect again— God is faithful in bringing light to even the darkest of moments, thoughts, and feelings. What former things do you need to let go of in order to rise up and move onto the new things God is showing you, calling you to, or doing in your life?

Prayer: Divine Creator, when I find myself trapped in the wilderness of the past, give me the courage to follow your lead into the light and be cocreators of the path to new life and resurrection. Amen.

Kate E. Smith

⌒ A Prayer for Renewal ⌒

My cup is empty. My spirit is less willing than it once was.

God, help me remember why I wanted to do this in the first place. How can I speak up when I feel as though I've screamed until I lost my voice? Help me feel your presence in this dry and barren wasteland. I don't know what I need anymore, but I trust that you can provide. Hide me away and protect me, so that I can find restoration. Pour your oil of reassurances over my head. Unclench my jaw, loosen my vise grip, and release the weight of the world that I'm holding. Today, give me rest, Comforter and Healer.

Tomorrow, give me the strength to stand back up and speak truth, life, and justice. Clear out my eyes so I can focus on the path in front of me. Shake the dust off my feet that had slowly turned to thick, hard mud. Place your almighty breath within me, so that when I speak up, and I will speak, there may be no more doubt around me. Today was not my day. And that's OK. For tomorrow holds new mercies, new promise, and new life. God, hide me under your wings, so I can emerge renewed, revived, and ready. Amen.

Katie Black

*Two men remained in the camp, one named Eldad, and the other
named Medad, and the spirit rested on them; they were among
those registered, but they had not gone out to the tent, and so they
prophesied in the camp. And a young man ran and told Moses,
"Eldad and Medad are prophesying in the camp." And Joshua
son of Nun, the assistant of Moses, one of his chosen men, said,
"My lord Moses, stop them!" But Moses said to him, "Are you
jealous for my sake? Would that all the LORD's people were
prophets, and that the LORD would put his spirit on them!"*

—*Numbers 11:26-29 NRSV*

Someone asked me, "I mean, who reads the Book of Numbers?" I knew
it was a rhetorical question, but I found my hand sheepishly creeping
up. My response, "My call story is in Numbers," elicited a sort of pleasantly
befuddled head tilt. I've since found this to be the standard reaction.

The first time I heard the story of Eldad and Medad, I had to pull my car
over because I couldn't drive and cry at the same time. I felt called by God
but I wasn't sure exactly what I was being called to.

God told Moses to gather seventy elders and bring them to the Tab-
ernacle. The Spirit of the Lord descended, and they all prophesied—one
translation says, "spoke the truth of God." Eldad and Medad were two of
the seventy, but they didn't go to the tent. They stayed in the camp. They
prophesied in the camp. They didn't fit, and it freaked the hierarchy out.
(Hence Joshua running off to tattle.) But Moses's response is perfect. "I
wish that all the LORD's people were prophets." That is one of my favorite
images of the Kingdom of God: where all the Lord's people are prophets.

I come back to this story often. Sometimes I am Eldad and Medad whom
the outsider people don't know how to handle. Sometimes I am one of the
sixty-eight, doing the expected duties so others can bring a word from a
new quarter. I am sometimes Joshua, imposing my limits on who does and
doesn't get to speak for God (which usually correlates to people I do and do

not like). On my best days, I get to be Moses. At my best, my leadership helps people find what God wants to say through them, offering it to the world from wherever they are.

Where I fit in the story changes, but the call it has formed in me never does. The voice of God is not limited to a select few. There is a word of God's truth in every person I meet. The world needs all those words, even mine. When I am tired or afraid, that helps me find the strength to speak. When I am frustrated by disagreement, it reminds me that mine is not the only voice of value. It keeps me dreaming and working for a day when prophecy runs beautifully amok; a day when everyone speaks the truth of God.

Prayer: God, help me find your voice, both within my heart and in the words of others. Give me wisdom and courage to speak your truth until the day when it reigns for all. Amen.

Kate Walker

Be strong and courageous, and do the work.

—*1 Chronicles 28:20 NIV*

The Holy Spirit never told me about the meetings that would drive me to sob in the parking lot or the infuriating conversations about the seemingly unimportant drama of the everyday. She never told me about the time when I would be called a bitch in the middle of a Trustees meeting, be told I was "bringing too much Jesus to church," or about the countless times that I was questioned about my sexuality because I was a single female serving in "a man's world." The Holy Spirit didn't tell me, when she was whispering my call to ministry into my ear, about all of the times when I would feel like I was not enough, or about how many times I would question whether or not I had any right to be heard.

Even though the Holy Spirit never told me these things . . . she continues to whisper in my ear. She continues to remind me that my calling is not from my congregations, my communities, or even from my denomination. My calling is, and will always be, from the God who created the universe— who set order to chaos—who has and will always partner with the lost, the last, and the least.

The Holy Spirit reminds me to be strong, to be courageous, and to do the work: the work that God has called me to do, and the work that calls me to partner with the lost, the last, and the least. The Holy Spirit reminds me that my true identity in Christ overcomes all the burdens, the drama, the gossip, and the "stuff" of us sinful humans that gets in the way of doing the work.

The Holy Spirit, she is funny. But she is who strengthens me, who pushes me to be courageous, and who gives me the fighting chance of doing the work. Sometimes that feels like the burden—but I am strong, I am courageous, I am doing the work because the Holy Spirit whispers in my ear and reminds me who I am, who called me, and that the work is not the "stuff." The work I am called to do is to partner with the lost, the last, and the least. We find our voices by claiming that work, today and every day.

Prayer: Holy Spirit, breathe into me your words, give me my voice. Help me do the work. Amen.

Gabrielle Marie Martone

"Now what have I done?" said David. "Can't I even speak?"

—*1 Samuel* 17:29 NIV

Before David can ever face the giant, he has to face his detractors—the people who still think of him as the youngest son with the lowest-level job, the people who have watched him grow up but are still not convinced he's grown, the people who have his best interest at heart but no longer know his heart. David's eldest brother, Eliab, hears him speaking to the soldiers, asking why this Philistine should have power over the people of God. Eliab rebukes David for being there at all, much less opening his mouth.

David's response is exasperated, frustrated, and honest. David asks, "Can't I even speak?" It's a question to his brother—will you allow me to speak? I think it's also a question to himself—can I do this? Can I find my voice to own my call, my story, and my gifts in front of those who know me best?

Before we can break stained glass ceilings, we have to defend our call to our families. Before we can hold court or run for office, we have to prove that we can handle it to our colleagues. Before we can be activists, we have to learn to tell our story to our friends.

When I was called into ministry, I was not convinced women could be pastors. I was quiet, shy, unsure of myself, and uncomfortable in my own skin. But God kept calling my name, inviting me to speak the truth. Not the truth that I had found, but the truth that found me. The truth that found me was that God can and will use anybody. The truth that found me was that God gives us all gifts to be used for Kingdom work. The truth that found me was that God would bolster my weak knees and steady my quivering voice. The truth that found me was that God's love is so all-embracing that I needed to be all-embracing too.

Somehow, perhaps because God opened God's mouth first by calling my name, I opened my mouth and started speaking truth.

There are many days I am still not sure if I will be able to find the words. There are many days when I get tongue-tied and wonder, "Can't I even speak?" It's then that the truth finds me again: that God calls me, that Jesus loves me, and that the Spirit equips me.

Prayer: Holy God, open my lips that I may speak. Unstick my tongue that I may declare the truth that keeps seeking me out and won't let me go. Clear my throat that my story may be heard. Amen.

Brandi Tevebaugh Horton

A Prayer for Moving Through Depression

O Beloved, you are deep and wide as you meet me at the margins of my experience, the depths of my mind and soul. I have been so low, the lowest and darkest points I have ever known. Thank you for the gift and grace I receive every day as I take my medication. Thank you for lifting up the floor to meet my feet so I cannot go any lower. You called me into the unknown, and I followed, hoping that where you were leading me there was abundant life. Now I am here and I know: it does exist. The floor is even higher and I know. Thank you for medication. Thank you for my family. Thank you for inviting me to heal and to know what it feels like to rise again. Amen.

Melissa Engel

A Prayer for God to Change the Way We Use Scripture

Most Holy and Welcoming God, grant us the courage to embrace what is and let go of what was. Give us the strength to deny using your word to clobber your beloved people,[10] to refuse to perpetuate discrimination through mistranslation of Scripture, and to seek a future of full inclusion for all as the whole body of Christ. May we condemn nonconsensual sex at every turn and embrace the varied and diverse spectrum of consensual sex embodied by your people and by your own creation; in your loving, inclusive name we pray. Amen.

Caitlin Simpson

*LORD, how long will I call for help and you not listen? I cry out
to you, "Violence!" but you don't deliver us. Why do you show me
injustice and look at anguish so that devastation and violence are
before me? There is strife, and conflict abounds. The Instruction
is ineffective. Justice does not endure because the wicked surround
the righteous. Justice becomes warped.*

—*Habakkuk 1:2-4*

It is beyond frustrating when you ask someone a question and they do not answer. When they sit there and just look at you, as if you had not even spoken a word. I can imagine the courage it took for Habakkuk to speak out to God in this fashion. Habakkuk was frustrated with God and tired of the silence and seeing the injustices happening in the world around him. Instead of being silent about how the prophet was feeling, we read here how Habakkuk found his voice and cried out to God.

I remember the day I found my voice to speak out against injustices. I received a text message from an attorney who was connected to a community center where I had worked. One of the young men had been beaten by police officers the night before and was out on bail. The days that followed were filled with listening to stories of the injustices that happen every day. Injustices that my white privilege had kept me from knowing about. A few days later, I found my voice when I had the courage to speak out against police brutality at a press conference held at the community center.

Have you ever been frustrated with God for not answering your question? Are there injustices you see happening around you that go unanswered, leaving you to wonder why God does not just fix them? Could God seem silent to us because we don't like God's answer? Could God be saying that the answer is within us?

Maybe the reason God has not come to the rescue is because God already put us in the situation to cause the change that is needed. Maybe God is trying to give us the courage to find our voice.

Prayer: Loving Creator, I am so quick to get angry and frustrated when I think you are not answering when I call. Help me remember that you are with me in those moments. Help me find my voice and have the courage to use the voice you have given me to speak up against injustice; in the name of the one who created me, redeems me, and sustains me I pray. Amen.

Rebecca L. Laird

*When they told Mordecai Esther's words, he had them respond
to Esther: "Don't think for one minute that, unlike all the other
Jews, you'll come out of this alive simply because you are in the
palace. In fact, if you don't speak up at this very important time,
relief and rescue will appear for the Jews from another place,
but you and your family will die. But who knows? Maybe it
was for a moment like this that you came to be part of the royal
family."*

—Esther 4:12-14

Sometimes, God calls us from places of comfort to places that are not so comfortable.

Even being a woman in ministry can sometimes be one of those places.

When I found myself in a place of comfort with a congregation who listened to me and heard God speaking through me, sometimes saying the really hard truths became a place of discomfort.

I knew that I was in a place where the people I was preaching to were not necessarily ready for a message of inclusion and love. They were not ready to be fully inclusive of their siblings in Christ who are LGBTQ+. But God laid it on my heart to preach that message.

But speaking the truth that God lays on our hearts is the reason we are called. Perhaps this is "such a time." We see in the wider world that people are hurting. We see on the news reports of assaults, discrimination, children being taken from their parents, mass shootings, police violence . . . and sometimes the church can be the place that we safeguard ourselves from that outer discomfort.

But we are called to such a time as this. We are called to speak a message of freedom, safety for all, healing, and overall peace.

So how can we find peace when we have such a discomforting call?

I think one of the most peaceful things is hearing God's call for myself. And although acting on that call can be hard and uncomfortable, knowing that I am fulfilling a call that benefits the greater kin-dom of God can bring me inner peace.

And not following that call, knowing that my family through Christ is in sackcloth while I sit in a king's castle . . . sometimes that in itself is even more uncomfortable.

So as we follow our uncomfortable calls, let us remember that we were called "for such a time as this."

Prayer: Dear God, when you call me into discomfort, remind me that you call me into your love. When I feel stress, remind me that you have a greater purpose. When it feels like my comfort is at stake, remind me that following your voice is more comfortable than any castle; in your life-giving, peace-filling name I pray. Amen.

Kelley Fox

～ **A Prayer for Vision** ～

Near One,
When I turn my eyes from you,
when I get wrapped up in wants and worries,
when I miss signs of your presence,
when I turn my eyes from other people,
when I numb myself to the pain of my neighbor,
when I miss opportunities to love and be loved,
when I lose sight of that place deep within where you guide me,
when I stop trusting that you are the source of my voice,
my vision, and my call,
O God, open my eyes.
Give me light to see as you see,
to see to the heart of things,
to see to the heart.
Amen.

Alison VanBuskirk Philip

Cultivating Peace

Conflict and peace are often seen as opposites—as if peace depends upon the absence of conflict, and the presence of conflict means there is and will be no peace until the conflict is done away with. Peace and conflict, however, are much more intertwined and interconnected.

Novelist N. K. Jemisin explains, "True peace required the presence of justice, not just the absence of conflict."[1] As we seek true peace—in our lives or in the world—we might find ourselves faced with more conflict than we expect. Whether it is because we are enforcing personal boundaries or are seeking dignity for others, conflict is often peacekeeping's dance partner.

In many cases, peace is the result of conflict, and is born from war. Peace is coming together for reconciliation. But it is not stagnant; it is dynamic. Peace brings us closer to others and seeks to break down walls; it seeks to bring people together and not separate us.

Peace doesn't mean we put up with other people's crap, either. Peace isn't about being nice. In fact, we bring about more peace facing conflict and addressing discord. Sometimes, we might bring more peace by walking away from situations so that we can have peace in our own lives.

Peace is personal, and it is global. It is a dynamic force calling us constantly into greater relationship with God, with one another, and with all creation. The prophets write about shalom—peace that includes justice, reconciliation, and wholeness for all humanity. Jesus promises peace for humanity as he heals, as he preaches, and even unto his death. This "peace of God that exceeds all understanding" is our greatest pursuit and our most divine calling (Philippians 4:7).

The reflections and prayers that follow seek to remind us of the many ways we can cultivate peace in our own lives and in the world. The stories told and the incidents that unfold in the pages ahead remind us that conflict and peace dance together to bring us closer to God's vision for our lives and for our world.

J. Paige Boyer

*Faithful love and truth have met; righteousness and peace have
kissed. Truth springs up from the ground; righteousness gazes
down from heaven. Yes, the LORD gives what is good, and our
land yields its produce.*

—*Psalm 85:10-12*

My phone vibrates, so I pick it up to look. It's an e-mail. From a
church member. I click on the notification, and it simply says, "Pastor, I'd like to come by and talk with you about something." My heart
starts racing as I frantically replay the past week. What are they upset
about now? Did I say something that ticked them off? I brace myself for
the impending meeting because I know it can't be good.

We've all been there. No matter where you work or serve, at some point
you've had an angry person at your door. For many of us, our instinct in
these moments is to keep the peace, to calm and to placate everyone so that
the tension goes away. Quickly.

But is that really peace? Or is it just a facade, polite pleasantries mas-
querading as peace? The work of peace*making* requires us to dig deep and
examine our roots, not just to smooth over the surface layer. Peace cannot
happen without a commitment to this laborious, even dirty, work.

As a gardener, I love the poetic imagery the psalmist offers us: faithful
love and truth meet, righteousness and peace kiss, truth waters the ground,
and righteousness shines from above. And then there's a plentiful harvest
of that which is good. The psalmist paints this beautiful picture of God's
kin-dom bursting forth when all the right elements come together—love,
truth, righteousness, and *peace*.

This word *righteousness* can also be translated from the original Hebrew
as "justice," or God's vision for those who are oppressed and marginalized.
And in Hebrew, "peace" is *shalom*, which is the life-giving idea of wholeness and restoration for both individuals and communities. So perhaps another way to understand this psalm is as a divine vision of the incredible

51

good that happens when righteousness that is justice and peace that is shalom come together. It's a vision of what happens when we do the hard work of peace*making* instead of peacekeeping. This psalm points us to a world made whole.

I think about that meeting again. And I begin to prepare. With love. And truth. And righteousness and peace. I was wrong—it can be good.

Prayer: Creating God, I've often heard the mantra, "no justice, no peace," but I confess that the words seemed merely a protest chant. I failed to see the divine wisdom in them, to recognize the biblical truths they echo. Help me resist the temptation to choose the easy way of peacekeeping and instead dig deep to do the hard work of peacemaking. Plant in me the seeds of your vision of love, truth, peace, and justice coming together so that your kin-dom can burst forth. Amen.

Mary R. W. Dicken

Jesus was in one of the towns where there was also a man covered with a skin disease. When he saw Jesus, he fell on his face and begged, "Lord, if you want, you can make me clean."

Jesus reached out his hand, touched him, and said, "I do want to. Be clean." Instantly, the skin disease left him. Jesus ordered him not to tell anyone. "Instead," Jesus said, "go and show yourself to the priest and make an offering for your cleansing, as Moses instructed. This will be a testimony to them." News of him spread even more and huge crowds gathered to listen and to be healed from their illnesses. But Jesus would withdraw to deserted places for prayer.

—Luke 5:12-16

Sometimes, I just need to lock myself away—not necessarily to pray, but just to be. The noise of the world and the weight of its needs—expressed in tiny voices and e-mails that just keep coming—drown out what I need. I go into overdrive to care for everyone else, to bring them peace, and, all too often, I have nothing left for me.

During those times, the Jesus I need is the thirtysomething-year-old guy who just needed to get away. Jesus wanted to heal the man with skin disease, wanted to raise life from death and feed the masses, and . . . all of that wanting occasionally wore him out. So, he went off by himself to pray.

I want to bring peace and healing to others too—through touch, through relationship. Living like Jesus means I also need to notice when I am touched out and need to seek peace for myself.

It is holy to step away for a time. It is faithful to focus on ourselves, to cultivate our relationships with God. And, like Jesus, we can return to teach and touch and heal when we are renewed—whether its after five quiet minutes or a week away from it all.

Prayer: Nurturing God, thank you for showing me that it's OK to step away. When I am touched out, loved out, moved to continue giving but desperately close to empty, guide me to the deserted place where I will find rest, peace, and renewal in you. Amen.

Shannon V. Trenton

A Prayer for Someone Who Is Hard to Love

Adoring God, I know you created all of us and that you love all of us, but there are days when I wish you would have made everyone just like me. It would be a lot easier to love my neighbor if they always behaved and believed like I do.

Please give me patience. It is beyond me right now. Give me your eyes of love to see the goodness you have given each of us, so I can love another with your heart.

I ask for your blessings on this person that I find hard to love. Today, maybe I am praying because I know it is the right thing to do. Tomorrow, help me pray this prayer in earnest.

Change my heart, O God, so I can support this person. Deepen my capacity to love them. Help my heart to be as limitless as your grace for this person and your grace for me. Amen.

Heather Dorr

A Prayer for Tough Conversations

May the Spirit speak, and may we acknowledge her voice.
May we know when to abide in silence, and when to give voice to the unexpressed.
May we come with hearts prepared to share in vulnerability and trust.
May the peace of Christ be present in the midst of uncertainty, fear, pain, and grief.
May our courage give birth to understanding, vision, and love. Amen.

Kate Mackereth Fulton

Therefore, I say to you, don't worry about your life, what you'll eat or what you'll drink, or about your body, what you'll wear. Isn't life more than food and the body more than clothes? Look at the birds in the sky. They don't sow seed or harvest grain or gather crops into barns. Yet your heavenly Father feeds them. Aren't you worth much more than they are? Who among you by worrying can add a single moment to your life? . . . Therefore, stop worrying about tomorrow, because tomorrow will worry about itself. Each day has enough trouble of its own.

—Matthew 6:25-27, 34

Sisters in leadership, it is my fervent wish that these verses from Matthew are thoroughly sufficient when it comes to snapping you out of your worst anxieties. I pray that these words are enough to assure you that the future will take care of itself; that the God who feeds the sparrows and clothes the lilies is watching over you; that all shall be well.

But what if you are one of the forty million American adults who struggle with an anxiety disorder? What if you're like me—someone who often finds that no amount of reassurance is enough to completely silence the racing thoughts of my fretting brain?

I was fourteen years old when I was diagnosed with an anxiety disorder (Obsessive-Compulsive Disorder, specifically), and I have spent more than half my life learning to live fearlessly and faithfully in spite of my brain's natural tendency toward anxiety. It's not easy. As you might expect given my vocation as a pastor, I've spent a great deal of time trying to discern how to faithfully follow Jesus's words here when my mind is working overtime to yank me in the opposite direction. Here is what I've concluded: even if your brain is programmed to worry, you can still follow Jesus's command to seek the Kingdom of God without fear.

So how do you do this when your overactive "fight-or-flight" reflex is being triggered multiple times a day?

You follow your treatment plan. You take your medication. You visit regularly with your counselor. You receive love and support from the unanxious people around you. You practice excellent self-care. You practice mindfulness, and you learn to be gentle with yourself and your thoughts. You take things one day at a time; sometimes even one breath at a time.

Dear sisters, we live in anxious times, and even those who are not prone to chronic worry often find themselves fearful about the state of the world around us. So regardless of your specific brain chemistry, I want you to know something: you are loved. You are enough. And things will be OK, even if it doesn't feel like it right now. The same God who tends to the needs of the birds and the flowers is on your side.

So breathe, courageous woman. Just keep breathing.

Prayer: God of the sparrows and the lilies, you know the fears that trouble my heart and mind, and you are at my side even in my darkest moments. Teach me to remain rooted in the present, empower me to care for myself and those who need me, and remind me that your peace surrounds me . . . even when I struggle to feel it. Amen.

Emily Spearman Cannon

Holiness is the union we experience with one another and with God. Holiness is when more than one become one, when what is fractured is made whole. Singing in harmony. Breastfeeding a baby. Collective bargaining. Dancing. Admitting our pain to someone, and hearing them say, "Me too." Holiness happens when we are integrated as physical, spiritual, sexual, emotional, and political beings. Holiness is the song that has always been sung, perhaps even the sound that was first spoken when God said, "Let there be light."[2]

—*Nadia Bolz-Weber*

I spent too many years warring with myself. My skin was too dark, hair too kinky, hips too wide, and mouth too sassy. I was too Black. As a teenager, I was repeatedly told that I needed to be more ladylike and poised. I was too wild. As a young adult, I felt the pressure to fit within the proper prototype of being a "nice, southern Christian woman" in order to marry a nice Christian man. This all meant that I was not *holy* enough.

One day I was walking down the street and got a glimpse of my reflection in a store window. I barely recognized myself. I had physically, emotionally, and spiritually morphed into someone that I did not know. My reflection seemed more like a window into someone else's life, but not my own. These were not my dreams, nor my hopes. This was not my voice, and this was not the life that I wanted for myself.

Right there, at the busy intersection, I began to weep. I wept for all of the years I questioned my worth because of racism and harmful European beauty standards. I wept because of all of the times I sat in church pews repenting of my sexuality because of bad theology about pleasure and purity culture. I wept because I listened to the serpent's voice that made me doubt that I was a beloved child of God.

I stood in front of my bedroom mirror and made peace with my body. I looked at my reflection and spoke words of love, affirmation, and healing.

I sang songs, danced, lovingly touched myself, and held my beautiful voluptuous melanated body without shame. I let love and grace wash over me like the redemptive waters of baptism. On that day, the thirty-two-year war against myself ended and "it was good."

Prayer: Dear God, thank you for the peace that comes from realizing that I am your beloved child. When I am at war with myself, remind me that I am created in your image. When I am confronting systems and theologies that go against your truth, send me friends and voices that speak your deeper truth. Amen.

Theresa S. Thames

A Prayer for Being Grounded/Present

God of silence and cacophony, of perpetual motion and stillness,
of chaos—the holy and the unholy kinds alike,
of time—then, now, and not yet, help me be where I am.
By the power of your presence,
help me be fully alive and present in this moment,
with body, mind, and spirit unified
rather than trying to go in many different directions,
as I am prone to do. Help me be where I am.
When I am overwhelmed by the too much-ness of life,
ground me in this moment, this place, this body.
As I seek to still myself, to lean into your presence, I breathe deeply.
As I inhale, I invite you in, God. Fill the worried regions of my mind.
Renew the exhausted areas of my heart.
Invigorate my body for action, for love.
Before I exhale, God, I cling to you.
Rather than entering for just a breath, dwell within me.
Linger so long that I begin to recognize a spaciousness within me
and the truth that I have ample room for you.
Occupy the corners of my spirit that were empty
until I welcomed you home into me again. As I exhale, I follow you, God.
It's not that you are departing from me,
but rather that you are leading the way to the next moment,
the next breath, the next age,
the next way you have prepared me to be used for building your kin-dom.
Before I inhale again, God, I surrender to you.
I recognize myself as depleted without you.
I long to follow you that I might be filled by you again.
God, you are the breath that carries me forward.
Let my every breath be a prayer.
Holy One, help me to always be where I AM. Amen.

Karen Hernandez

Your word is a lamp to my feet
and a light to my path.
I have sworn an oath and confirmed it,
to observe your righteous ordinances.
I am severely afflicted;
give me life, O LORD, according to your word.
        —Psalm 119:105-107 NRSV

I can't read the words of Psalm 119:105-107 without the saccharine tones of mid-eighties Amy Grant echoing through my head. As a decidedly uncool, youth-group kid in high school, I could croon "Thy Word" with enough angst to match any New Kids or 'NSync fan. I matured into an appropriately jaded twentysomething, and the song came to represent a juvenile faith blissfully ignorant of the realities of the world. But in my thirties, sitting alone on a crowded plane, I longed for that kind of assurance.

Discipline, faith, and obedience had seemed to foster success; good grades, good job placements, a good family. Yet internally, I felt far from good. What depression didn't numb, anxiety exacerbated into impossible obstacles. I was stalked by the fear that one day someone would figure out I wasn't joking when I frequently said, "I'm a terrible person." Then the whole facade of hard work and shiny accomplishments would crumble.

I was flying to a leadership retreat designed for young creative professionals trying to do courageous and innovative work. A mentor had suggested I apply, but I remained convinced that not one of the words in that description applied to me or the work I was able to do. I was out of my depth and looking for a verse of Scripture to practice artsy lettering in the hopes that it would make me feel both calmer and more creative. I came to Psalm 119:105-107 and the old refrain wafted through my head. Then my eyes kept scanning down, resting on verse 107: "I am severely afflicted; give me life, O LORD, according to your word" (NRSV). Here was a kindred spirit. I started at the top and took in the whole psalm.

There is tension. The verses of praise and self-promotion are punctuated by pleas for rescue and reassurance. Psalm 119 is not sugar-coated optimism. It is the record of a long, internal struggle between faith and despair. Apparently, impostor syndrome is not a new problem.

I am sometimes tempted to treat Scripture like a leadership handbook or a checklist for success. God reminds me it is more. Peace comes not from adherence to every detail, but from realizing I am not alone. Leaders have struggled and felt inadequate before. God carried them; God did great things through them. God has called me and will do the same for me.

Prayer: God, when I am lost, your word is my light. Guide through the dark seasons of my life and revive me when I am weary so that I might offer your life to others. Amen.

Kate Walker

Finally, brothers and sisters, good-bye. Put things in order,
respond to my encouragement, be in harmony with each other, and
live in peace—and the God of love and peace will be with you.

—2 Corinthians 13:11

We live in a world filled with so much unrest. We don't have to look far to see violence, fear, and pain all around us. The words of the apostle Paul, as he concludes his writings to the church in Corinth, seem to ask something of us that can often seem impossible. Order, harmony, and peaceful living—where do we even begin to start with all that is happening around us? Being a peacemaker amidst the chaos of the world isn't easy work.

As I open my e-mail each morning and read news alerts, the work of peacemaking—of being in harmony with one another, of trying to bring order amidst chaos—seems so far out of my reach. How can I make a difference? Where do I even start? Those questions swirl in my mind as I learn more about the hurting people of the world.

In Matthew's gospel account of Jesus's birth, the world then seems so similar to today's. Herod's fear and jealousy turned to violence and brought chaos to Jesus's family and all of Israel and the surrounding areas. Jesus came amidst that fear and jealousy, violence and chaos, as the hope of the world. Jesus broke forth as the hope amidst a world full of unrest. Jesus continues to break into our world as the hope amidst all that goes on.

As I wrestle with the daily news alerts and struggle to find my role in making a difference in doing the challenging work of peacemaking, I always have to remember that peacemaking is not my work; it's God's work that I get to be a part of. None of us are doing this work on our own. Jesus continues to break forth into our world as a bright light of hope, peace, and love; and it is only because of Jesus that we can even begin to do the hard work of peacemaking, and as Paul reminds us, "the God of love and peace will be with [us]."

Prayer: God of love and peace, as I look at my community and beyond, I am overwhelmed with all of the pain and chaos in the world. It's hard to know where to begin as I seek to live into your call to bring peace and order. Thank you for not letting me do that work alone but for being the hope and peace that not only moves me to action but also guides and encourages me in that hard work. Draw me ever closer to you and into your work of peacemaking. Amen.

Jessica Lauer Baldyga

A Prayer for Choosing Peace Instead of Vengeance

O God who is always working for peace, there are so many times in life when I feel overwhelmed by the terrible situations around me. This world can be so unfair, so awful, so broken. Many times, it seems that those horrible situations are aimed right at me. In fact, it seems that there are people who have it out for me, who are seeking harm for me or those I love.

When I experience the evils of this world, help me, O God, not to seek revenge, but to choose instead to cultivate peace. This is difficult, and I'm not sure that I would be able to choose that decision. Please guide me, direct me, help me make the choice to work for peace.

Joseph chooses peace as he forgives his brothers; just as he put aside an instinct to seek vengeance, help me do the same. Remind me, just as you did Joseph, that when others seek evil, you are intending to create good.

Stir up within me a desire for a more holy way. Stir up within me a more tender heart that reflects your love. Stir up within me your perfect peace and help me bring it to fruition in my life and in this world.

Amen.

Nicole Wiedman Cox

When you pass through the waters, I will be with you;
when through the rivers, they won't sweep over you.
When you walk through the fire, you won't be scorched
and flame won't burn you.

—Isaiah 43:2

Balance—I often find myself struggling to find it. It feels elusive. I know I'm not alone in this. I often feel like I'm failing in every area of my life. On a good day, I know perfection is impossible to attain—we can't keep all the plates spinning at the same time. On a bad day, perfectionism takes over, and I feel like a huge failure.

Sometimes, balance is not an option: when I had a miscarriage, when I awaited test results, when I suffered from depression, to name a few. There have been many times when I felt I was drowning—in grief, fear, pressure, shame, never-ending to-do lists. . . .

One day when I was feeling particularly defeated, I went to see my spiritual director, and she opened her Bible to Isaiah 43. The words washed over me like a healing wave. Each word renewed my spirit and gave me strength to persevere.

On this journey, I have hit walls, I have had scares, I have been in pits that felt insurmountable, I have faced adversity—and every time, I come back to Isaiah 43. Each of these words wrap around me like a shield of God's loving protection. They build me back up again to face a new day, because I can't let this world knock me down. There's too much life to be lived and love to be felt and shared.

I hope that when you face the worst life has to offer, you also remember these words: When you pass through the waters, God will be with you. God is with you—always. When you walk through the rivers, they will not sweep over or overcome you. You will not get lost in the sea of whatever it is you are going through. God is with you. God will not let you go down.

When you are walking through the fires of life, you won't be scorched.

The world may do its best to try to scorch your dreams and squelch your passion, but God is not going to let you burn. Keep your focus on God, the giver of gifts, the one who calls you.

Prayer: God, it's not easy out here. Sometimes I feel like I'm drowning. Help me keep going. Sometimes I feel like the flames are too hot, and I'm going to get burned or burnt out. Shield me; help me persevere. When everywhere I look there is adversity, help me see you. Give me your strength, your guidance. And let everything I do be for your greater glory. Amen.

Julia Singleton

Then one of the elders said to me, "Who are these people wearing
white robes, and where did they come from?" I said to him, "Sir,
you know." Then he said to me, "These people have come out of
great hardship. They have washed their robes and made them
white in the Lamb's blood. This is the reason they are before
God's throne. They worship him day and night in his temple,
and the one seated on the throne will shelter them."

—*Revelation 7:13-15*

L ess is more. Or so they say.
  Look less this or sound less that. Do less of this and take up less
space. Eat less. Sleep less. Speak less. Think less.

For all these things, the world promises to reward me. With love. With
affection. With adoration. With wealth. With security.

Why can I not conform?

Inside, I am at war. With myself, with them.

I do the things I hate. Or rather, I do the things they taught me to hate
about myself.

The glimpses of beauty and peace that I know are who I am truly meant
to be have become blurred and blocked by who I have become or who I
have had to become.

I love less. Especially myself.

Because I know who I really am.

This is why I will never really conform.

Neither can I live this hardship, this pain, this distortion forever.

Who are you? They ask.

Sir, you know. I answer.

I am the good. I am the broken. I am the beauty. I am the searching. I am perfection. I am growing. I am big, small, wild, tame, quiet, loud. I am giving. I am receiving. I am free.

I am sheltered by love greater than any amount of less.

I am greater than the hardship of their life for me.

I am full of peace in spite of less.

I am more.

Prayer: Lord, grant me peace today in the face of all that brings pain, anxiety, and fear. Shelter me in the fullness of love that outlasts the smallness of human expectations. Make peace within me a possibility, a priority. Fill me with more. Amen.

Sarai Case

A Prayer When Facing (One's Own) Complacency with Oppression

Fearless Liberator, Beloved Reconciler, you would never walk away from someone in pain. I need freedom from the past and forgiveness for the present. I have seen my neighbor dying by the roadside. I recognize the blows of oppression in . . .

> the destruction of black and brown bodies.
> the detention of immigrant and refugee bodies.
> the expulsion of LGBTQIA+ bodies.
> the antagonism of impoverished bodies.
> the condescension of disabled bodies.
> the eradication of indigenous bodies.
> the derision of our female bodies.

I heard their voices. I saw their wounds. I averted my eyes. I did not stop. I walked on by.

Maybe I was busy.

Maybe I was burnt out.

Maybe I was trying to survive myself.

So I passed them by, offering "thoughts and prayers" instead. I knew better than this, but I did it anyway. I was consumed with my own failure and embarrassment.

Fearless Liberator, Beloved Reconciler, undo this self-preservation. Never let me use differences of identity or experience stop me from helping others in need. And when my own failure to be a good neighbor is brought to light, give me the self-compassion to confront my own inner demons, so I can confront the trauma of this world. Like Fannie Lou Hamer, may I always recognize that "nobody is free until everybody is free."[3] Most of all, thank you for taking my hand from this ditch I have placed myself in. Amen.

Hillary Taylor

The truly happy person
doesn't follow wicked advice,
doesn't stand on the road of sinners,
and doesn't sit with the disrespectful.
Instead of doing those things,
these persons love the LORD's Instruction,
and they recite God's Instruction day and night!
They are like a tree replanted by streams of water,
which bears fruit at just the right time
and whose leaves don't fade.
Whatever they do succeeds.

—Psalm 1:1-3

I know I am called to be a peacemaker, but I cannot even seem to find peace within myself. I live with so many tensions about my vocation, my role, my work, my relationships, the increasing polarities in political culture, the elusive "balance" in life. And brokering (or even encouraging) peace in a world full of people so determined to assert themselves through oppression, conflict, and violence would be a monumental task on its own!

It might be helpful to work on my own inner peace if I want to bring peace to the world. I'm not likely to resolve much of my own tension by working harder or reading the latest self-help book. So I turn to Scripture, and I find one of the most peaceful images in the Bible in the very first psalm: a tree planted by a stream, bearing fruit at just the right time—not too early, not too late; a tree whose leaves never fade; a tree that succeeds at everything it does.

I have a deep longing to be this tree, with just enough nourishment, never too much or too little, bearing exactly the right fruit at the right time, staying bright as the day God made me, never fading under the pressure of so many ideas and expectations.

At first glance, it appears the psalmist is suggesting I might be that perfectly peaceful tree if I am completely faithful to the law of God, if I avoid sin altogether. And reading this, the stress creeps back in. It looks as if I can only achieve such peace if I work harder and follow the law perfectly (something I know I cannot do).

Looking more closely, people who are like these trees are not those who strictly follow instructions, but those who love and delight in God's word. They don't swim across the river as fast as they can, thinking about the next holy task, but instead take time to wade into God's word, splashing around in that holy stream, laughing and lolling about on the sunny banks, sitting still long enough to hear when God speaks.

Those are the happy, fruitful trees, the ones who delight in God. Those are the people who find peace.

Prayer: God of all things, in the midst of my turbulent life, help me take time to delight in your word, and to allow you to plant me by a peaceful stream, where I might learn to be a peacemaker after all. Amen.

Elizabeth Ingram Schindler

Turn away from evil! Do good!
  Seek peace and go after it!
                    —*Psalm 34:14*

Peace means so many different things to different people. Some people have told me that you keep the peace by ignoring anything that would bring about conflict. For others, they say that in order to seek peace you've got to do anything you can to bring about liberation, even if it makes people uncomfortable at times.

I tend to find myself more in the second category of folks. Which is how, one summer while attending seminary, I found myself serving as a faith-based community organizer. One day, while working to rehab a house to make it into a community center, the woman I was there with pointed out the .22-caliber bullet hole in one of the back windows of what would become the reading room for children. I remember thinking that evil is present in this world. There is still peace to pursue, but sometimes the culture can be so rooted in destruction that it's hard to see hope, let alone know what we can do about it.

Chasing after peace didn't end for me after that summer; if anything, it had just started. Today, that looks like having hard conversations about the world we live in with people who don't always agree with me. It means educating about God's idea of peace that calls people to a radically new way of living because of our faith.

Recently, one of my great-aunts passed away. As my dad offered a eulogy at her funeral he said two things that struck me. First, she was a woman who was known by the fruit of her life, including peace; and second, she was a rebel. The peace that my aunt had wasn't the peace that avoided conflict, instead it was the peace that called for radical transformation and living a life that worked to bring about God's vision of shalom.

The thing about seeking peace is that it's hard work. It's hard to turn away from the evil that just seems to captivate this world. It's hard at times to do good, again and again. That's what makes cultivating peace a radical act—but something that the psalmist reminds us that we are to go after!

Prayer: God of peace, we confess that we have often overlooked your vision of shalom that calls us to be people of liberation, setting it aside for the sake of our own comfort. Forgive us, Lord. Renew in us your vision of wholeness and send us out, not just to proclaim it with our lips but to seek after it with our lives; in your name we pray. Amen.

Michelle Bodle

⌒ A Prayer for Fearless Leadership ⌒

Gracious God, you have called me from death to life. In years past, you gave me direction, a purpose, vocation, a call.

In previous seasons I was energized, optimistic, hopeful about possibilities for the future. But I must confess that this world is bigger, heavier, more oppressive than I realized in my younger years.

My body is not my own. My rights are being eroded. My sisters' voices are still being silenced and swept away.

I am weary. But underneath my weariness, if I am honest, is fear.

Fear that my call to serve you was a pipe dream.

Fear that what you sent me to do is going to be impossible.

Fear that the daily pressures of life have silenced my ability to speak your truth.

Fear that the call to lead that you have placed upon me is too much for my inadequate self.

Free me, O Lord.

Free me from the trappings of my own mind and heart as they whisper lies about my ability to lead.

Free me from caring about those who would rather I be quieter, or "just a little less intense."

Free me from the lie that my leadership doesn't make a difference.

Free me for joyful obedience, for it was you who called me to be a fearless leader, to preach the good news in all I do, to be a steady presence for those I love, to reach out to my circle of loved ones when I am unsteady, to tell the truth in love.

And may my fearless leadership—the role you have called me to—call out injustice, push brokenness into the light, cry out for restoration of all the world, and name your peace as the reality we seek to create together.

I ask for your guidance as I step into the unknown and claim the role of fearless leader—the role you have called me into. In Christ's name. Amen.

April Casperson

An angel of mercy on horseback with a box of firecrackers in her saddlebag. My picture of Miss Henderson was more and more intriguing.[4]

—*Catherine Marshall*

I spotted a young man walking down the stairs, a gun strapped to his side, an obvious open carry. This was the first I'd noticed, but his choice to carry had been agitating others for over an hour. It took every ounce of energy I had to remain calm, as I tried to deescalate a near-shouting match. On one side, a veteran emphatic that he would not feel safe where a gun was present. On the other, the young man defending his Second Amendment right and his intent to protect his family.

It became evident that no one was interested in my pleas to remember that we worship a Prince of Peace. The young man kept insisting that he would protect his family at ALL times, and in all places, fearing an active shooter situation. Eventually the conversation went from white hot to stony silence as opposing parties left through separate exits. Standing alone, my heart shattered as I realized this young man was so trapped in fear that he only felt safe when carrying a weapon.

Trying to keep my tears at bay, I remembered Miss Alice, my favorite fictional mentor. Miss Alice, a Quaker missionary in Cutter Gap, Tennessee, finds unexpected ways to engage the people in this Appalachian community. "The Cove" is plagued by poverty, Typhoid, feuds, and long-standing grudges—conflicts that are often solved by gunfire. The threat of death is constant, and the fear gripping the community is evident.

Miss Alice learns to shoot a rifle, perfecting her shot, and earns the community's respect. And yet, this compromises her beliefs, nearly breaking the boundaries of her values. She cultivates authentic relationships by getting on their level, "speaking their language," showing mercy, love, and grace in abundance while addressing the fears at the heart of Cutter Gap's feuds and grudges.

When fear runs rampant, may we remember to approach tense situations with creativity, curiosity, grace, and love instead of reaching for "the rules" or our own expectations of the "right" way to resolve a conflict. By doing so, may we build authentic relationships, meeting people where they are, and lay foundations of peace, necessary for building the kin-dom of God.

Prayer: God of Compassion and Grace, help me see and love people as they are and where they are. Give me imagination to see things from their perspective and empower me with empathy to feel their pain and sorrow. Then give me the strength and mercy to extend your peace to them, even if they seem unready or unwilling to receive it. Amen.

Katharine L. Steele

"Can God set a dinner table in the wilderness?" they asked.
—Psalm 78:19b

I am a sucker for a pretty tablescape, especially picture perfect ones in magazines and on Instagram. They simultaneously inspire me and make me feel like a failure in my own home because we ate in front of the TV again last night. Yet, I know beautiful things can happen around a table, regardless of what it looks like . . . the trick is remembering that.

The table is a place where I have brought my greatest of joys and deepest of griefs, a place where friends have shared life-altering news, a place where I have shared in triumphs and failures. As I get older, I am continuously reminded that it's less about the way the table looks and more about who gathers around it.

In my life, I feel called to fight for a table big enough for everyone—goodness knows that this gets messy. Yet God has shown me time and time again how important gatherings at the table, rooted around food and community, are to creating the kin-dom here. A dinner table in the wilderness calls for creativity and flexibility and pretty much guarantees the unexpected will happen. This is where the beauty is, where the possibility lies, where we are not in control and stop trying to be. I truly believe that the table (wherever it is) leads to wholeness, creates welcome, urges peace.

My prayer is that you remember to trust in the beauty of the unknown, working toward connection in the wilderness of your life. It's not what the table looks like, but who is welcome around it.

So, may we never stop inviting others to share a meal, never stop talking about the hard things in life with friends and strangers, and continue to eat food that brings joy.

Prayer: Welcoming One, you extend your table wide and open your arms wider to each of us, regardless of who we may be or what we may have done. Help me trust in the possibilities that begin around your tables. May I continue to grow your welcome table and build your kin-dom here. Amen.

Catherine Jordan-Latham

∼ A Prayer for Yet Another Snow Day ∼

Dear God whose name is Love, Scripture says that one day for you is like a thousand years, and today, I think I finally understand how that can be. The immensity of your love seems even more miraculous now. How have you put up with us and our bickering for actually thousands of years?!? Wow.

Save me, O God, from my energetic children and their cabin fever. Grant them the ability to play well together, or at least near each other, for more than five minutes at a time. Do not take away the power, or the heat, or the Netflix. May we not run out of snacks; for they, I believe, are the source of all joy. I have been blessed by these tiny humans you have entrusted to my care; bless me once more with extra-long naps and abundant hot chocolate.

Warm my heart, O God, and warm the air, just a little. Grant me the hope that school will eventually, someday, open again.

Amen.

Allie Scott

When the angel came to her, he said, "Rejoice, favored one!
The Lord is with you!" She was confused by these words and
wondered what kind of greeting this might be. The angel said,
"Don't be afraid, Mary. God is honoring you." . . . Then Mary
said, "I am the Lord's servant. Let it be with me just as you have
said." Then the angel left her.

—Luke 1:28-30, 38

I have always imagined this moment as stereotypically heavenly: bright lights, kind and gentle voices from both Gabriel and Mary, and a quick and straightforward exchange. But I also wonder if, instead, it was frightening and confusing. I wonder if Mary felt vulnerable, scared, and alone. Her life as she knew it was going to change. The world as they knew it was going to transform.

I wonder if Mary knew that her *yes* was literally going to result in her carrying and birthing Peace into the world. A census was being taken (and if it was anything like today, used to divide between those who are of worth and those who are not). An insecure leader was constantly lashing out, trying to prove that he was powerful. I wonder if Mary's personal world was full of conflict and turmoil. Perhaps some wondered about her life choices, questioned or accused her.

Just like the way that I used to think about this biblical text, I thought that being a peacemaker or cultivating peace is about keeping a calm tone, soothing anger, and creating a heavenly atmosphere. There is value in having a calm voice and an ability to defuse tension, but it is not the only way or tone that is needed to cultivate peace. It is possible to cultivate peace in the thickest of tension, when I am frightened, scared, or confused. Cultivators of peace step into the unknown, say yes by speaking truth to power, calling in injustice, and screaming from the top of our lungs.

Racism, sexism, ageism, homophobia, xenophobia, and so many other ways in which harm is done are everywhere. For me, sometimes frustration turns into anger, which turns into exhaustion, which finally ends in surrender. But I am reminded that my calling is not to surrender; my calling is to follow Jesus Christ, the Prince of Peace.

I am grateful for Mary's *yes*. During a time filled with tension, fear, confusion, and pain, she carried and delivered Peace into the world. May we cultivate peace by carrying the fire of peace within our bellies and delivering it into wherever there is injustice.

Prayer: Prince of Peace, I confess that I am scared, frightened, and confused when I hear, witness, and experience injustice. I confess that at times I find it easier to ignore it or walk away. Thank you for your gift of peace. Help me carry peace and bring it into places where it is needed. Amen.

Bich Thy (Betty) Nguyen

*They were to bring Queen Vashti before him wearing the royal
crown. She was gorgeous, and he wanted to show off her beauty
both to the general public and to his important guests. But Queen
Vashti refused to come as the king had ordered through the eu-
nuchs. The king was furious, his anger boiling inside.*

—Esther 1:11-12

*N*o. It's such a small word. With such power.

How many have endured pain and abuse until that one day they
have had enough, and they utter that simple, strong word that changes everything? Vashti ended a cycle of drunken coercion and control by refusing
to follow the orders of a king. She reclaimed her life by saying no. What
peace must have come over her, even as the king's anger boiled inside him.

No is not a word we see as cultivating peace. In fact, many women avoid
it for fear of causing discord. I am a people-pleaser. I don't want to say no to
joining another committee for which I don't have the time, because I don't
want to let anyone down. But there are other people I know, many of them
women, who are afraid that saying no to someone would rain down violence upon them. They believe they must keep the peace, even when what
they are living is not true peace. Vashti's story reminds us that the word
no can be liberating—even when it brings an end to relationships. Her no
enabled her to avoid the pull of someone else's expectations—expectations
that were abusive.

What if we said no to that next expectation, whether it's a new work
project for which we won't get paid, or the next dieting craze, or staying in
a relationship with someone who does not respect us? Wouldn't we find a
bit more peace within ourselves when we stop putting ourselves on display
for others?

There are consequences to saying no, of course. Vashti's story in Scripture ends with her banishment. From what we see of King Ahasuerus, banishment from his presence is a good and beautiful thing. But it also makes

the king scramble for more control, and so more women—girls really—are swept up in his quest to find someone who won't say no to him. He doesn't find her, not exactly. Esther plays into the expectations presented for her when Vashti refuses, but she ends up using those expectations to manipulate the king. I don't believe Vashti regretted stepping away from those expectations though. Wherever she was in her banishment, even if her life was harder in some ways than it was in the palace, I believe she was at peace, knowing she made her own way.

Prayer: God, give me the courage to say no to expectations that do not give me life. As you strengthened Vashti, so strengthen me to stand up for myself and, in so doing, find peace. Amen.

Shannon E. Sullivan

⌒ A Prayer in the Midst of Division ⌒

God of all people, I am overwhelmed with the divisions I see in our world. The polarization, the conflicts, and the schisms weigh on my shoulders. I feel the constant pull to choose sides when I don't always fit completely on either side. I long for middle ground and acceptance. I yearn for understanding and fruitful conversations between people.

Help me work toward unity, while reminding me that unity does not always mean that I must agree with my neighbors. Guide me with your Spirit. Increase in me an ability to discern when I should let go and when I should speak out—when I should choose a side and when I should reach out to both sides. Give me strength to love people even when we disagree.

Open my eyes to see the gifts you have given to each person. Open my heart to help me understand others. Open my mouth to speak truth.

Amen.

Katrina Paxson

He asked a third time, "Simon son of John, do you love me?"
Peter was sad that Jesus asked him a third time, "Do you love
me?" He replied, "Lord, you know everything; you know I love
you." Jesus said to him, "Feed my sheep."

—*John 21:17*

I backed into a car, causing a wreck in the McDonald's drive thru. Right on cue, the driver sprang out of her car, screaming at me. To be fair, I did deserve that. But the passenger also got out, and gave me a look that said all too clearly, "This isn't about the car."

As the driver's rage released, it felt like my Monday couldn't get worse. Suddenly, her anger spilled into grief right before my eyes. She admitted that she only went to McDonald's to get herself some real food. She finally felt secure enough to tear herself away from the hospital, where her son had been treated for a gunshot wound over the weekend.

My guilt stretched the length of Texas. There I was, complaining to myself about my dumb mistake and moaning about Mondays. And there she was, a mother trying to get back to her injured son. Without thinking or forming a plan, I did something I had never done before. I asked, "Are you praying people? Can I pray for your son?"

Instantly, she broke into a smile and reached out her hand to mine. Peace, grace, and forgiveness flowed between us. I held hands with the women I had just harmed and let God repair a small piece of the damage I had inflicted that morning. We connected.

I had never felt so small. Or so guilty. And yet, through the mistake, I saw Jesus in her instant forgiveness and grace. She embodied peace in that moment while we prayed, even though she had reason for rage. I can only hope to be as gracious as she was right after the worst day of her life.

She was like Jesus, restoring Peter. Do you love me? Feed my sheep. I went to McDonald's for food, but instead, I crashed into Jesus unaware.

Prayer: Holy Spirit, be so near to me that, even on my worst day, I can still reflect your grace. Allow grudges to melt from my heart at the mention of your name. Create peace in my life, so that healing can occur within my very soul. Amen.

Katie Black

Come, see the LORD's deeds,
  what devastation he has imposed on the earth—
  bringing wars to an end in every corner of the world,
  breaking the bow and shattering the spear,
    burning chariots with fire.
"That's enough! Now know that I am God!
  I am exalted among all nations; I am exalted throughout the
  world!"

  —Psalm 46:8-10

The world began as chaos. In the deep waters there was only abyss, until God called from it every living thing. God set things in order. Yet at every turn, chaos is trying to creep back in. As often as humans try to put it right, entropy is always increasing. Chaos is always trying to make a play to take back the universe.

My thoughts often sound like chaos. Following one thread of thought ends up multiplying into a dozen. I don't just start one project, I start twenty. I flit from one idea to another. I get caught up in negative self-talk. I struggle with these thoughts day and night. How am I going to get it all done? Am I disappointing my family? Am I enough? How will I pay the bills? Did I remember to turn the stove off? It circles faster and faster and faster until I'm exhausted, dizzy, and sleepless for days on end. It requires intervention.

In Psalm 46, we witness God calling it all to a halt. I imagine God to be like the Supremes with their iconic opening choreography to "Stop, in the Name of Love," but instead the lyrics are God saying "That's enough! Now know that I am God!" and it is enough. It's enough just to know God. It is enough to stop the hurricane of thoughts. It is enough to stop the torrents of self-doubt. It is enough to clear a path through the muck in my mind to sit and be. And so to each thought I say, "That's enough!" and after many rounds of back and forth, the torrent subsides. The art of meditation has helped me find myself a calm, quiet center that does not ask so many questions. I listen to the truth that God has ended wars and can bring peace to the chaos of my mind.

Prayer:
It is enough to know God.
It is enough to know God.
It is enough. Amen.

Sarah Karber

∼ A Prayer for When Your Mental ∼ Health Makes You Feel Insufficient

Everything is just "a lot," God, and today I simply don't feel good enough.
My mental health has left me feeling small, insecure, broken, and lost,
and I wish I could get up and get out;
I wish I could dance in the sunshine
and sing with the bluebirds,
but it's all just
a lot.

On days like today, I struggle to find you
and grace and love seem just beyond my reach.
You remind me to "be still, and know that I am God."
Yet in this moment, stillness brings shadows,
and knowing you feels impossible.

So even if it feels impossible right now,
I believe (even if I do not know)
that you come and sit with me in the shadows.
I believe (even if I do not know)
that you pour out your grace on my neurotransmitters:
through medication and therapy,
through long walks and deep breaths,
through good food and cool water.
I believe (even if I do not know)
that you fill me with your resilience,
and in this moment I can be still
and know I am yours. Amen.

Laurel A. Capesius

When Joshua was near Jericho, he looked up. He caught sight of
a man standing in front of him with his sword drawn. Joshua
went up and said to him, "Are you on our side or that of our
enemies?" He said, "Neither! I'm the commander of the LORD's
heavenly force. Now I have arrived!" Then Joshua fell flat on
his face and worshipped. Joshua said to him, "What is my mas-
ter saying to his servant?" The commander of the LORD's *heav-*
enly force said to Joshua, "Take your sandals off your feet because
the place where you are standing is holy." So Joshua did this.

—Joshua 5:13-15

For the Israelites, coming out of the wilderness must have been a joyous celebration with a terrifying aftermath. It took forty years of communal preparation for this rag-tag nation to move into a new country, only to discover that their adversaries, the Canaanites, were still alive and well.

According to the Book of Joshua, the Canaanites are the ultimate Other: they pose a threat to the Israelites' safety and identity as God's chosen people. And according to the Israelites, God wanted the Canaanites eliminated from the land. But does the request to annihilate the Canaanites really come from God, or does it come from the prejudices of the Israelites themselves?

Joshua 5:13-15 challenges the idea that God wants the Israelites to commit full-throttle genocide on the Canaanites. Consider Joshua's simple inquiry about taking sides. Joshua doesn't know it, but he's essentially asking God's representative (the commander of the Lord's army) which side God is on. The commander refuses to be aligned with the Israelites or the Canaanites. Instead, he simply proclaims that the presence of the Lord is near, and that Joshua should remove any barriers between himself and God immediately. It's a moment of pause and worship. It's a moment where Joshua is made to wonder, "Is it more important for God to be on OUR side, or for us to be on GOD's side?" With these actions, the commander seems to implicitly say, "Remember, O Israel, you are more like the Canaanites than you could possibly imagine. So before you wage war with them, be aware. You may be waging war on your very selves."

Our conflicts might look different if, just before battle, we would pause and ponder the thoughts of our Creator. We can't always avoid conflict, or even right and wrong. Not everything in this world is just. But how do our battles grieve God? Perhaps this pause, this pondering the heart of God, perhaps it would shift our mindset from "us" versus "them" and into compassionate voices for change.

Prayer: Holy Confronter, you make human beings more alike than different. When we are tempted to divide others into camps of "us" versus "them," help us make room instead for our common humanity. God, you come alongside each and every one of us to unite us in the family of creation. Help us live into your truth, especially when we are tempted to see the Other as the Enemy instead of as Our Neighbor. Amen.

Hillary Taylor

*Don't let any foul words come out of your mouth. Only say
what is helpful when it is needed for building up the community
so that it benefits those who hear what you say. . . . Be kind,
compassionate, and forgiving to each other, in the same way God
forgave you in Christ.*

—Ephesians 4:29, 32

Can I be real for a moment? I wish Jesus-loving folk would pay attention to these verses from Ephesians and live them in our everyday
lives. Do not let foul words come out of your mouths, or through your
tweets, on your Facebook feed, or e-mail inbox.

I want it for you, but I don't always want it for me. When someone
hurts me, criticizes me, attacks my character, or even simply critiques my
grammar on social media, I am ready to wield my keyboard into a weapon
and destroy them with my words. Anger is my default emotion. It does not
take me long to realize that my anger is more about what's going on inside
of me. Somehow these words have tapped into a space of insecurity and fear
in my heart and mind, a place of pain and unwanted vulnerability. And if
I am not careful, I become a hurting person that hurts people. That's not
me and that's not you. We do not have to respond to hurt with hurt, harm
with harm. Jesus modeled another way: FORGIVENESS! "Be kind, compassionate, and forgiving to each other, in the same way God forgave you
in Christ" (Ephesians 4:32).

Forgiveness is first extended to ourselves. I have these mind messages
that attempt to speak what I call limitation prophecies over me: "Rachel,
you can't, you shouldn't, you are just not enough." These words have origins in people's mouths, e-mails, tweets, and make their way into my head
and heart. And sometimes I believe them. But then God, through Jesus,
reminds me: "Rachel, you are beloved!"

Forgive yourself for not living up to your preconceived notions of perfection. Forgive yourself for wanting what others have. Forgive yourself for

being a grumpy human most days. In the name of Jesus Christ, you are forgiven!

And now it's your turn—we are all in this together! I need your words of forgiveness, your words of encouragement, your words that remind me that I am who God and others say that I am. I need you. We need each other to remind us that we are beloved children of the living God.

Prayer: For all the $%@! that we talk about ourselves and one another. . . . In the name of Jesus Christ, you are forgiven; in the name of Jesus Christ you are forgiven! Glory be to God! Amen.

Rachel Billups

A Prayer for Parenting a Child
with Special Needs

Kind and Compassionate God, your perfect love casts out fear and anger, guilt and shame, grief and pain. But today, I feel all of these things. I grieve for my child whose special needs bring unwanted stares, insensitive remarks, and painful isolation. I worry for my child's physical health and social, emotional, and spiritual well-being. I feel guilty for lamenting the loss of the life I thought I would have, and I am ashamed for pushing others away because I feel my problems are more difficult to bear than theirs. I feel tired and weary from the physical, emotional, and spiritual demands of being a caregiver.

O God, soothe my heart with the healing balm of your presence—the very same presence with which you surrounded your son as he suffered on the cross. Help me experience your grace in the everyday things and to take each day one moment, one minute, one second at a time. Give me the strength to care for my child, and help me set aside time for myself, so that I may bask in your love and grow in my faith, refreshed and renewed for this journey I walk. Help me allow others to walk alongside me and to forgive those who mean well but who are unable to do so.

Loving God, turn my sorrow into joy—joy in the little victories that each day brings and joy for my child whom I love beyond description. Above all, fill me with your perfect love, so that my child will experience your gracious presence through mine.

In your holy name I pray. Amen.

Amelia Beasley

*This is the paradox of tolerance, the treason of free speech: we
hesitate to admit that some people are just . . . evil and need to be
stopped.*[5]

—*N. K. Jemisin*

When I think of peace, I don't think of quiet or tranquility. I think of what comes from the hard work of meeting those different from us and working together toward lives that are more harmonious—where our differences compliment and refine us instead of separating us.

Peace doesn't ever arrive on its own. Even as we pray for peace, God leads us into *action* to bring about that peace.

I have learned to bring about peace in my life and community by using my voice. On one hand, free speech is amazing and can be used to speak much-needed truths into the world. It gives me the right to express my opinions about myriad things from biblical interpretation to LGBTQ+ rights and more. I have certainly benefited from being able to say all the things I want to say—even the things I look back on and regret, like old blogs and tweets from days past.

Here comes the hard part about free speech, though: it also gives others the same rights. Some use that freedom to spew what I know to be incorrect, extra-factual, and downright offensive. There are, indeed, limitations to free speech. But for the most part, free speech allows for a whole multitude of sins.

In a world where free speech is running roughshod over peoples' identities, freedoms, and personhood, peace might require us to rethink what it means to have that kind of freedom and how we ought to make use of it.

True peace requires us to use our freedoms to stand up for those whose voices have been trampled, lifting them up and calling them forward. We must use our voices to shout over hateful speech; our hearts to heal those broken by the words of others; and our hands, feet, and wallets to make it clear that peace won't be overcome by hate-filled rhetoric.

Peace comes from the freedom we have in Christ to be advocates for justice. The freedom we have as those redeemed by God's love calls us to act for the redemption of others. Our peace comes not at the expense of another's peace but because more people can know God's peace—not through freedom of speech but through freedom in Christ.

Prayer: God of Shalom, living into your peace does not call me to be quiet. Instead it calls me to raise my voice above the fray and to increase the voices of others. May I listen for your words and your ways as I seek peace in this world. Amen.

J. Paige Boyer

Sun

make me whole again.[6]

        —*Audre Lorde*

We fall apart.

    Sometimes, when life happens, we fall apart. Our bodies get tired. Our minds scatter. Our will gets weak. Our relationships fail. We fall apart. *Discombobulated* is a good word for it: strewn all over, confused, and disconcerted, we need something or someone to come and pull our act together, pull us together so we can go and pull everyone and everything back together.

I have a bad habit of being the "strong friend." I make sure I'm available for my friends, as we all do. My bad habit is hiding when I am in need. When I'm hurting or afraid, I hide it from my friends. I try hard to hold it together around my family. I don't want to burden them with my emotions or my stress. I hold it in. I catch myself holding it all together.

Every now and then, I fall apart.

The cracks in my armor begin to show. I stop seeing myself as an Amazonian superhero and begin to worry about my frail humanness. I worry that, in seeing me fall apart, my friends and family will think I'm weak or incompetent.

Instead, they think I'm human.

I was never actually meant to hold everything together. Neither were you. Your back isn't broad enough. Your shoulders aren't strong enough. It's OK to let things go. You give your attention to so many things. Your family. Your faith. Your friends. Politics. Professional obligations. Personal goals. You deserve to focus on yourself. You deserve to take the time to see all of your pieces, all of your parts, and love them.

Though it may sound cliché, there is power in nature to pull you back together.

Breathe.

Let the energy of the sun love your pieces back together.
Breathe.
Let the warmth of the sun love your scattered parts back together.
Breathe.
Let the light of the sun love you from discombobulated to whole.

Prayer: Sun, make me whole again. Lord, I know that you hold all my pieces in your hands. No matter how scattered my mind gets, you know. You know me. You know what I need. You know everything I need to do. Please pull me back together, back to you. Please send your energy, your warmth, and your light to even my innermost parts that I might know peace in the midst of life. Make me whole again, not that I may be superhuman but that I can be who you made me to be and do what you created and called me to do. Thank you for never requiring that I hold it all together. Amen.

—Brandee Jasmine Mimitzraiem

~ **A Prayer for an Abortion** ~

God,

You already know all I have been through to get to this point.

You know every hair on my head.

You have been with me as I carefully weighed the choices before me.

You have been with me as I imagined a multitude of futures.

You heard my cry for clarity.

Be with me now, in any pain I may feel, physical or otherwise.

Guard my heart that the privacy and intimacy of this decision would not turn into secrecy and shame.

Remind me that you care much more about me than whether my womb is full or empty.

Remind me, when I feel like nothing is the same anymore, that your love remains constant, unchanging, and steadfast.

Remind me that I am yours and beloved by you, now and always.

Amen.

Amanda Baker

Facing Loss

From the first book of the Bible, we encounter women who face loss over and over again: the loss of community, the loss of children, the loss of their own voices. Eve's son's blood calls out to her from the ground, and the only response the text gives her is the naming of a third son. Hagar might not lose her life, but God still sends her back into slavery. Sarah fades from the story before her death; we never know what she thinks of Abraham taking her child away to be sacrificed. And Rachel's dying words proclaiming her loss are stifled as her husband changes the name of her son from Benoni, son of my suffering, to Benjamin. Throughout the Bible, when women endure loss, they are not permitted to speak the truth about suffering.

We feel our losses are also stifled, even thousands of years later. We are taught to cover up our losses, to not let anyone know how sick we really are, to not mention that miscarriage, to stop crying already. We are admonished with a litany of "at least," reminded that someone else always has it worse, and denied the truth that our loss is real. And we are told to look for the silver lining. That every storm is followed by a rainbow. So suck it up and move on.

No.

When we approach loss like this, we become isolated. We start to believe our grief is a moral failing or a hormonal imbalance rather than the truth of being human. We start to believe that we are truly alone, that no one else has mourned the loss of a love that might have been or a relationship that was once lifegiving but has since become toxic. We wonder if we are the only ones who have feared for our health or safety.

We forget that God can take our pain—indeed that God experiences our pain alongside us. In this section, you will find honest reflections from women who refuse to face loss alone. You will read raw honesty—sometimes uncomfortable honesty—and you will hear the voices of women who refuse to suffer in silence anymore. Instead of silence, they offer their stories to you so you don't feel so alone. And as a reminder that it's OK not to be OK.

Shannon E. Sullivan

When Mary arrived where Jesus was and saw him, she fell at his feet and said, "Lord, if you had been here, my brother wouldn't have died." When Jesus saw her crying and the Jews who had come with her crying also, he was deeply disturbed and troubled. He asked, "Where have you laid him?" They replied, "Lord, come and see." Jesus began to cry. The Jews said, "See how much he loved him!"

—John 11:32-36

They didn't get it. They thought Jesus's tears were for Lazarus. Why would Jesus bother to cry over Lazarus? He told his disciples Lazarus was dead before they even got to Bethany. He let it happen. He planned all along to resurrect Lazarus from the grave. Why would he bother to grieve someone who would be alive within minutes?

It was Mary that moved him. She made him bend down in tears. He felt her grief and anger. He saw her weeping and wept with her. Even knowing that the story wasn't over, he paused in the midst of her sorrow to sorrow with her. Jesus did not cry for Lazarus . . . he wept with Mary.

We can meet Jesus in our grief. Like Mary, we say, "Lord, if you had been here. . . ."

Jesus pauses . . . Jesus weeps. He is moved by our sorrow. Yet, he does not rush to fix all that is broken or to resurrect all that is dead. Instead, he stays with me and weeps with me.

God's work is not only about resurrection and miracles. This is God's work: sitting and weeping with the brokenhearted and loving you when you are bitter that God didn't save this day from coming. God allows you to be angry when God seems too late.

In just one chapter, Jesus will go to the cross and on his way he will stop in Bethany. Mary, her tears now dry, will care for him as he prepares for his tomb. Others will not understand. They will criticize her gift as too much. But Jesus will accept her extravagant gift, just as he accepts her broken heart. Jesus weeps with us as we weep.

Jesus is here, and he is moved by your tears. Jesus weeps with you. There may be more to come in your story . . . but not now. Now is the time of weeping.

Prayer: Jesus, if you had been here! My heart is broken and my tears burn in sorrow. Weep with me, Lord. Let me know that you have not deserted me to cry alone. Open my eyes to see how you love me. Amen.

Crystal Jacobson

In Joppa there was a disciple named Tabitha (in Greek her name is Dorcas). Her life overflowed with good works and compassionate acts on behalf of those in need. About that time, though, she became so ill that she died. After they washed her body, they laid her in an upstairs room. Since Lydda was near Joppa, when the disciples heard that Peter was there, they sent two people to Peter. They urged, "Please come right away!" Peter went with them. Upon his arrival, he was taken to the upstairs room. All the widows stood beside him, crying as they showed the tunics and other clothing Dorcas made when she was alive. Peter sent everyone out of the room, then knelt and prayed. He turned to the body and said, "Tabitha, get up!" She opened her eyes, saw Peter, and sat up.

—*Acts 9:36-40*

It's OK to be mad at this story in our sacred text and throw your Bible down in bitter sadness as you read the happy ending of Dorcas coming back from the dead. As much as I believe (or want to believe) in an all-powerful God, I know my loved ones aren't coming back. Peter no longer travels around raising people from the dead.

While I have seen the power of God work physical miracles in people's lives, I also know that's not happening *this* time. And it's not fair. The women who loved Dorcas cried out to Peter and he brought her back. Do my cries mean nothing, God?

I know God's heart breaks with mine. In my most honest moments, I know wishing someone back from the dead is more for me than for them.

As the numbness of loss slowly fades and God gently coaxes me back to life, I have learned not to focus on the end of this story. Hope and truth don't come from Dorcas's rising for me anymore but, instead, from how beautifully this woman's life made a difference in so many others. The first thing we're told about her is "Her life *overflowed* with good works and compassionate acts" (Acts 9:36b, emphasis mine). Though she was gone from this world, the love and goodness she poured into the lives of others was still very much there. The widows showed Peter the tunics and other clothing Dorcas had made for them when she was still alive. Can't you just picture them: tears in their eyes as they clung to the work of her hands, holding up the physical evidence of her love?

At most funerals, things the deceased made and loved are on display, sharing something that holds a little bit of their essence with the mourners.

Every time I go through the back door of our house, I touch and hold the screen door that my husband's Aunt Jojo helped him install. Though she left us too soon, a little bit of her is there, ushering us in the door. Her love lingers as the work of her hands welcomes us home. And I like to think she'll be there herself one day to welcome us to our next home.

Prayer: God, losing people I love sucks. It never gets easier. It never makes sense. Help me cling to their love still surrounding me. Amen.

Corey Tarreto Turnpenny

⌒ A Prayer for Disappointment ⌒

Empty, Lord—I am empty. The space and place in my soul that was once filled with hope and future is now empty. Disappointment is stealing my joy. Can't you feel my dry soul?

I am weary, Lord, so very weary. Just when I felt like things were falling into place, the pieces I set with care are now scattered—strewn about and broken. There is no way to put them together again. Disappointment is stealing my future. Can't you feel my scattered soul?

Alone, Lord, am I alone? The path mapped out before me is now cluttered with misfortune. Every corner brings frustration, every hope is crushed. Disappointment is stealing my spirit. Can't you feel my heavy soul?

God of the empty and weary and lonely, renew my vision so I might cling to your hope again. Take the broken pieces and bring resurrection. Restore hope as I live in your promise. Give me your peace, to find your Spirit here—in the emptiness, weariness, and loneliness of disappointment, knowing that even here—you are with me. Amen.

Katie J. P. Bishop

When this perishable body puts on imperishability, and this
mortal body puts on immortality, then the saying that is written
will be fulfilled: "Death has been swallowed up in victory.
Where, O death, is your victory? Where, O death, is your
sting?" The sting of death is sin, and the power of sin is the law.
But thanks be to God, who gives us the victory through our Lord
Jesus Christ.

—1 Corinthians 15:54-57 NRSV

Often we talk about struggling with illness as a battle that is won or lost. If a person is healed from their disease, they win; they defeat their foe. And if a person succumbs to their illness and dies, they lose their battle. When my mom was first diagnosed with cancer, I knew she would beat it. She was strong, healthy, and relatively young. She had already overcome many other challenges in life, and cancer would just be another problem to be solved. She fought valiantly through surgeries, radiation, and chemo. Though her determination did not wane, her condition worsened.

I resisted the imagery of losing a battle as I watched my mother fight against her illness. Even as her own body struggled against her, she got up every morning to take my twelve-year-old sister to school. Every weekend, she put on her fuzzy cap and ventured out to watch middle-school basketball games. She pushed herself farther than was physically possible each and every day. How could I talk about her losing a battle?

Throughout my mother's illness, I prayed for a cure, I prayed for healing, I prayed for a miracle. As her condition changed, my prayers changed with it. I began to pray for victory. In this passage from 1 Corinthians, we are given powerful imagery for life beyond death. God offers victory in the face of loss and death. Death is not a defeat; disease and illness do not win. Illness has no power over the body, and death has no power over life in God's eternal presence. God is victorious, and God gives us victory through Jesus Christ.

I knew my mom would beat cancer, and she did, just not in the way I had originally envisioned. My mother did not lose her battle; the battle ended, and she was victorious. She entered the presence of God, a place where disease cannot go and death does not win. Her mortal body put on immortality; her perishable body put on imperishability; and death lost its sting. Though I still miss my mother, I trust in God's promise that death is swallowed up in victory. I trust God's word that death, pain, and grief do not have that last word. I trust in God's victory for my mother and for all of us.

Prayer: Almighty and Eternal God, you promise to give your people victory through the Lord Jesus Christ. When I am facing loss, help me trust in your power to overcome death. Give me comfort now when I am mourning, crying, or in pain; help me know that, in you, someday all these things will be no more, and I will be victorious; in Jesus's name. Amen.

Jodie Ihfe

*"He will wipe away every tear from their eyes. Death will be no
more. There will be no mourning, crying, or pain anymore, for
the former things have passed away." Then the one seated on the
throne said, "Look! I'm making all things new."*

—Revelation 21:4-5a

I put the test in the trash . . . negative again. My back hit the bathroom
wall, tears streamed down my face. It was the ninth consecutive month
with a negative test. It was the time of year for miracle babies and virgin
births.

The cold tile corner of our parsonage bathroom was the perfect place to
fall apart. My husband tried to comfort me. We cried together.

Infertility is isolating. Reminders of my malfunctioning womb seemed
to be everywhere that Christmas. From friends' pregnancy announce-
ments, to TV commercials, to another holiday season of family parties with
well-meaning questions about when we would be starting a family. All of
these reminders of my empty womb left me feeling broken, marred, and
unworthy.

One sleepless night while journaling, I read Revelation 21:4-5a. The
tears began streaming down my face. In that moment, I realized that sometimes things fall apart before they are remade. That's what necessitates the
remaking.

That Christmas I fell apart, in a beautiful way. I quit trying to be perfect, and I quit trying to pretend everything was ok. I wept in my husband's arms. I rocked in my mother's embrace. I raged to the safety of my
father. I vented to my sister and even rejoiced in the gift of my newborn
niece. And, in the space, Jesus remade me.

I am still on the journey of being remade, as we all are. Infertility does
not define me; it does not define my marriage. It is merely a part of my
story. I would love to tell you that our journey with infertility has had a

happy ending. Even still, four years after falling apart that Christmas, we have no bundle of joy to add to our family Christmas card.

In fact, we are embarking on the journey of adoption. It's another step on the journey of being remade, another way God is making our lives new. I am choosing to step into the remaking, trusting that Jesus has the power to make even seemingly hopeless things new.

Prayer: God who makes all things new, in stillness and hope open my fragile heart. Give me the strength to allow you to begin to remake me. Amen.

Andrea Curry

*But we had to celebrate and be glad because this brother of yours
was dead and is alive. He was lost and is found.*

—Luke 15:32

While he was not a religious person, my dad nonchalantly told us one day that he wanted "Amazing Grace" to be played on the bagpipes at his funeral. He meant when he was eighty or ninety, and I envisioned the same.

The day after my daughter was born, I got a call that my dad had been admitted to the hospital. Many tests and procedures later, he had an emergency brain surgery. Not long after the surgery, early in the morning, after a snowstorm, he died at sixty-three years old. He was surrounded by his wife of thirty-five years and two of his three daughters. I was home with my newborn waiting for the snow to end.

In the weeks following his death, I was lost in the mix of joy and grief of having a baby and losing a parent side by side. I felt lost in the mix of gratitude that she was in my arms and sadness that she will never know him. I felt lost because my dad, who had represented stability to me, was gone, while I needed to be a source of stability for a new little life. Even though I felt lost, even though tears usually come easily for me, I struggled to cry.

We waited until summer to hold his memorial service, which gave me time to wade in the loss. It gave me time to be honest about my sense of guilt for not being present when he died. It gave me time to remember the love he had for me and the love I had for him, the kind of parent-child love I want my daughter to feel from me and for me.

As the bagpiper started to play to open his service, as the tune of "Amazing Grace" filled the air, my eyes finally filled with tears. The words, "I once was lost but now am found," rose in my head to meet the music. I had lost my dad, but in that moment I knew he was not lost. And neither was I. One of the prayers in the United Methodist funeral liturgy says, "Keep true in us the love with which we hold one another."[1] In the love with which we hold one another, we are found, held by God, held by a peace that passes understanding, forever.

Prayer: Lord of Life, may you hold me and all whom I love in your love, which is so strong not even death can hold it down. Amen.

Alison VanBuskirk Philip

God is our refuge and strength,
a help always near in times of great trouble.
That's why we won't be afraid when the world falls apart,
when the mountains crumble into the center of the sea.

—Psalm 46:1-2

When life is crumbling around me, and I feel I've lost control, God is there—strong and powerful, wanting to protect me. I find great comfort in that. In those moments, I try to rest in God's strong presence. Instead of frantically trying to do it all myself, I can take a deep breath and rest in the solid shelter of the Lord. I may still have to clean up a mess or rebuild the brokenness, but I don't have to stand all by myself. In God, I always have One who is wanting to care for me.

Three years ago, my mom lost her battle with cancer. It wasn't unexpected, but it was difficult. I deal with death often in my work, though, and thought I was doing pretty well with my grief. I weathered the first holiday season and felt surprisingly fine. But come January, I started to feel tired. I was exhausted. By early afternoon each day I could barely keep my eyes open. It went on for weeks, so I asked for prayers, and friends suggested I go to the doctor, thinking it was my thyroid. As I shared with the doctor it became so clear: it was not my thyroid; it was my grief. I wasn't sobbing all the time or having trouble eating; I was just exhausted. My words gave way to tears, and I started to feel better. After my appointment, I started actively grieving, and the fatigue lessened significantly.

As I reflected on that experience, I started to see more clearly that what I've described as "situational depression" in my life could also be called "situational grief." It isn't always death, sometimes it's a broken relationship, a failure at work, or unmet expectations. When life is painful, I often fall into feelings of helplessness, sadness, and lack a desire to do much, and I've called it depression. But I think, more than that, it's grief.

I need to honor the loss, to pray, journal, walk, or have some kind of catharsis. I need to lean into God. My grief may not ever cease, but by actively being aware of it, I can keep it from overwhelming me.

Prayer: God of mercy, grace, and healing, life can be so heartbreaking. When I keep experiencing loss, help me remember I can never lose you. When everything else is slipping away or falling apart, help me call on you to keep me safe and wrap me in peace. Through Jesus Christ I pray. Amen.

Debbie Sperry

⌒ A Prayer for the Death ⌒ of a Beloved Parent

Loving God, my earthly parent—the one who first showed me what it means to call you mother and father—has gone to be with you.

Now, God, I need you to be my parent as I weep and wail and mourn the arms that embraced me when I cried, the hands that held my own, and the voice that taught and guided me.

You may not have arms to embrace me, yet may I still feel your comfort enfold me.

You may not have hands to hold me, yet may I still experience your tender love.

You may not have words to heal me, yet may I still listen to your spirit moving.

Divine Parent, comfort me as my beloved parent becomes part of you. Help me feel their presence across eternity. Teach me to know that they are within me, even as they are within you.

God, I know they are not entirely gone. In their presence here, in their time with me, they have made impressions that will last forever and will carry me forward.

Even through my tears, loving God, I thank you for my parent—for the memories we made, the lessons they taught me, and the very gift of life that came through their love.

God, help me feel them—in this place and in this time, in every place and in every time. Amen.

J. Paige Boyer

What, do you wish to know your Lord's meaning in this thing?
Know it well, love was his meaning. Who reveals it to you? Love.
What did he reveal you? Love. Why does he reveal it to you? For
love. Remain in this, and you will know more of the same.[2]

—*Julian of Norwich*

I sometimes wish that I believed everything happens for a reason. It sure would be easier. We are meaning-making beings, so it's a natural inclination. Life would be a lot tidier that way. But I don't believe that.

I cared for a foster baby for almost a year and then said goodbye. This Julian of Norwich quotation was in the devotional I read the day she left. When I told people she was leaving, I posted it on social media to try to get ahead of the clichés and unhelpful explanations people often offer when they don't know what to say.

I understand that these clichés come with a desire to offer comfort, but I don't believe them. The best "reason" I had was this: the reason my foster daughter came into my life was love. The reason it was so hard for her to leave was love. The reason we crossed paths was so we could love her. That's about as much meaning as I can make of loss some days. Some days I can make even less.

On the hardest days, I don't cling to the idea that God is in control or that everything that happens is part of God's plan. If I did, some days that would make me very angry. Instead, I cling to the fact that God loves me more than I can understand. And God loves our foster daughter.

But that isn't really an answer. The end isn't the one for which I had hoped. But I know when I face loss and grief and pain that it wasn't to teach me a lesson, and I doubt that it's part of some grand plan. Can it teach me something? Perhaps. Might it be redeemed? I hope so. But what I know for sure is that, while I cry and grieve and scream, and maybe even cuss, God's love isn't going anywhere. And if I cling to that love, truly I believe that I will know more of the same.

Prayer: Abiding God, lead me into your love and remind me of your steadfast presence, whether I feel it or not. In the midst of clichés and hollow answers, help me abide in your love—even with all the other thoughts and emotions I may feel at that time. Let me know more of the same love that has brought me this far. Amen.

Katie Lloyd

Love endures and goes on, in spite of all the feelings of grief inside us.[3]

—*Joyce Rupp*

In the days leading up to my mom's death, my newborn son and I spent time with her. We knew we would have to say goodbye soon. While she was weak and bedridden, she could hold her grandson with some help and enjoyed any time we could spend with her.

I introduced Mom to the toy lion I'd just bought for the baby. She held it in her hands. Even though lifting her arms was challenging, she slowly but playfully trotted the lion over to her grandson. Despite her weakness, she found a way to lovingly interact with her youngest grandchild. Smiling, I thanked her. This moment of simple play touched me so deeply. I know I will continue to have an attachment to that toy lion long after my child outgrows it.

Before I left, I helped Mom hold my baby for what would be one last time. As we held him together, she repeated a single refrain, over and over again, words which I will never forget: "I love you . . . I love you . . . I love you." The words *I love you* can never be said too much. As my children grow, I am helping them know that love.

In the months since this beautiful moment, and since my mom's death, I continue to grieve, and I am constantly reminded of the love that endures beyond all space and time, for all of eternity. It is a gift from God which will never be surpassed. It is a comfort while on Earth and a hope for Heaven. Love overcomes so many things, bringing healing and peace. Thanks be to God.

Prayer: God who brings forth life and extends life beyond death, guide me with your gentle Spirit. Bring peace, comfort, and hope as I remember through tears and smiles, and as I carry on the love that was passed on to me. Amen.

Jennifer Zeigler Medley

⌒ A Prayer for Loneliness ⌒

God, there is so much emptiness in my life. Even when I am surrounded by people, I feel so impossibly lonely.

My life does not look like I thought it would . . . it is not filled with the people and relationships I hoped it would be. I look around and see the world moving on without and beyond me, and I wonder, O God . . . how did I get here? How do I move on from here? Why am I stuck here, in this place, feeling lonely and afraid? Remind me that even as I grieve what is . . . even as I long for what I thought would be . . . that I imagined my life would be . . . even then, I know you have come with me to this place and have never left my side.

Draw near to me, O God. Even when the world around me is full of pain, sorrow, and undistinguishable noise, you are with me, longing to comfort me.

Help me rest in that comfort and in your unwavering peace. For even when I don't *feel* your presence, I know that you are always there by my side as my ever faithful friend, companion, and guide. Help me trust in this promise, and in your embrace; in Jesus's name. Amen.

Jen Tyler

God heals the brokenhearted
 and bandages their wounds.
God counts the stars by number,
 giving each one a name.
 —*Psalm 147:3-4*

I have lost three pregnancies. Three babies. I have had two miscarriages and one ectopic pregnancy (which was by far the scariest and the most painful, emotionally and physically). Three children who are not. Three siblings to my living children.

When I think of facing loss, I think of facing the truth that three humans died inside of me, and I am the only one who ever knew them as living. I am not the only one who loved them. My spouse joins me in love of them, along with their grandparents, their siblings, and all who knew they were expected and did not arrive. Facing loss means facing the fact that I will never know them or hold them in my arms and that no one else will either.

When I read this verse from the Psalms, I know my babies are loved and known by God as they are by me. I have tattooed three stars on my back. Each one of them lights that have pierced the darkness. Each one of them the hope that I would be their mother: tend to their scraped knees, kiss away their tears, and hold them when life doesn't turn out as they had hoped and planned for.

Stars are the lights that pierce the darkness, especially in a new moon. I live in a city, but I remember camping out west where there were no city lights. I was there at the new moon standing under the vastness of the sky with more stars than I have ever seen before or since in my life.

This psalm promises what I already know deep in my heart. God knows each of those stars and names them. For those of us who have lost babies—whether six weeks in utero or six days of life or six months or six years or sixteen years or thirty-six years—God knows them too. God knows how new life is a promise that pierces the darkness. God knows how new life is hope and love and connection with something bigger than ourselves.

For all of us who have felt the emptiness when we should have been full, God names our children Beloved.[4]

Prayer: O God, for the losses I suffer that you know so well, give me peace. Help me know that though I cannot hold onto what is gone, you embrace what I cannot. Hold my losses close to your heart, count them and name them, love them as I have been unable to do. I give my losses to you, knowing that nothing and no one escapes your care and love; in your son's name I pray. Amen.

Emily A. Peck-McClain

"*I tell my students, 'When you get these jobs that you have been
so brilliantly trained for, just remember that your real job is that
if you are free, you need to free somebody else. If you have some
power, then your job is to empower somebody else. This is not just
a grab-bag candy game.'*"[5]

—*Elissa Schappell*

It was the first day of orientation, and I had found my person. We spotted
each other while awkwardly waiting in the lecture hall for the Dean to
deliver a welcome address. After the gathering, we gravitated toward one
another and began a journey of friendship that would sustain us throughout our graduate program. We were strangers who had become family. We
did everything together and supported one another through exams, heartache, natural disasters, and moments of joy. We committed to many years
of love and support for one another. Then things changed.

After graduation, we moved miles apart and began our careers, doctoral
programs, and living life. The phone calls and text messages became less fre-
quent, and there was subtle tension in every exchange. This tension surfaced
as we shared personal and professional achievements. The news of a promotion was met with questions about readiness, the giddiness of a new partner
was shadowed by reminders of failed previous relationships, and our reunions
felt like a competitive gathering of frenemies. As the gaps between calls and
meetings grew, so did the gaps in our friendship, which eventually ended.
There was no reason given, no closure sought. Things just changed.

When I think about the handful of friendships that have ended over the
years, it is mostly due to what I call scarcity theology. Scarcity theology
is the belief that God's blessings, goodness, mercy, and grace are limited.
This skewed view of God's benevolence leads to competition and jealousy,
and makes it nearly impossible to celebrate others as they persevere in life.
This theology is especially harmful to women as we engage in behaviors
and adopt attitudes that hold us back.

There are times when I miss my old friend, and I whisper a prayer on her behalf. What I've learned from the loss of our friendship is the importance of empowering everyone around me to live into their fullness. I have become mindful of when I am engaging in unhealthy competition, withholding resources, or feeling jealous of another woman's success. I now make it a point to extend hospitality, offer support, and to debunk the myth that women do not work well together. As Toni Morrison says, my job is to spread power and champion freedom.

Prayer: O God, you know your child and all of the ways I am driven toward achievement and success. When my selfish ambitions impede my ability to celebrate and encourage those around me, call me out and lovingly draw me in. When I face the loss of once life-giving friendships, teach me to find abundance in new ways. It is my sincere prayer that I live a life that testifies of your goodness, abundance, power, and freedom. Amen.

Theresa S. Thames

⌒ A Prayer for Moving ⌒

Gracious and Loving God,
I have felt your movement in my life,
and I have responded, once again;
here I am, send me.
For a time I have served you here,
in this place that has become familiar and comfortable.
Now, you are inviting me to step into the boat, to lose sight of the shore,
as I follow you into this new stage of my life.
I am excited about new possibilities;
yet in the midst of this joy, I grieve what I am leaving behind—
my family, my friends, the community I have grown to love in this place.

Help me remember that gone does not mean forgotten.
Help me in this bittersweet transition to know that you are here, in the midst of it all, in the midst of us all, always.

I give thanks for all that has been and all that will be.
I give thanks for technology which helps bridge any distance.
I give thanks for the Holy Spirit who brings peace in and around this tumultuous time.

In the name of Jesus Christ, who knows the anguish of saying goodbye to family and friends, I pray.
Amen.

Bethany Willers

Rachel died and was buried near the road to Ephrath, that is, Bethlehem. Jacob set up a pillar on her grave. It's the pillar on Rachel's tomb that's still there today. Israel continued his trip and pitched his tent farther on near the tower of Eder.

—*Genesis 35:19-21*

Someone I know and love, with a full-bellied laugh, is dying. Someone who had a terrible childhood and who helped build a beautiful one for me is dying. A man who struggled with addiction and taught me how to dance is dying. And I cannot control it.

I hunger for control. For order. It's helpful to have a plan, to know what the right thing is to do, to have a designated task, to have a role. What about in the face of loss? Death? What are we to do then? Though these verses aren't a command, or even necessarily instruction, they do offer a rhythm for grief; they do offer a path which leads "farther on." And, though these verses are brief, their brevity does not signal a quick process of grieving. We are allowed to walk the path at our own pace.

"Rachel died," they wrote. The authors of Genesis didn't parse words, because saying anything other than the truth in the face of loss is flimsy, unstable ground. The truth, at least, is real. Sturdy, no matter how heavy or jagged. This is step one: tell the truth about what is happening or what has happened.

After she is buried, Rachel's husband, Jacob, builds a pillar to mark the holy site, the sacred ground. Both burial and building are deeply physical acts. Burial and building pull us out of our heads and return us to our bodies. This is essential in the face of loss, because loss doesn't make sense, no matter how much we philosophize. Losing something, or someone, is terrible. And it doesn't make any sense. This is step two: do something physical, return to the body.

Israel journeys on. Israel is both Jacob's new name and the name for the whole people of God, communicating that Jacob is re-membered into the whole people of God, re-membered to his community after the isolating experience of loss. Israel journeys on. All together. This is step three: remember community. Remember that a community exists, even though loss convinces the griever that they are alone. Re-member that community, gather it together, join it anew.

Now, it is possible for Israel to move from the site and time of loss, to move "farther on." Who knows where they had planned to go? Israel just pitched their tent somewhere else. At some point, no matter how long it takes, we are given biblical permission to leave the scene of loss. You will continue on. I will continue on. Though it seems impossible, without that which we have lost, we will journey farther on.

Prayer: God of Rachel and Jacob, help my sorrow, anger, relief, dancing, building, and crying forge a path farther on. Amen.

Alexa Eisenbarth

LORD, you have examined me.
  You know me.
You know when I sit down and when I stand up.
  Even from far away, you comprehend my plans.
You study my traveling and resting.
  You are thoroughly familiar with all my ways.
There isn't a word on my tongue, LORD,
  that you don't already know completely.
You surround me—front and back.
  You put your hand on me.

—*Psalm 139:1-5*

I placed my hand on the curved, black, metal door handle after I navigated through the dark basement where I had slept the night before. It had been a night and afternoon that I would never want to revisit, in life or in my dreams. And yet, I did for the next month and a half. But there I was that morning: light was creeping above the Adirondack pine trees that were still snug in their blanket of fresh, white, glistening snow from the night we were just escaping.

As much as I wanted to crawl back into my bed and just rest after such an incredibly exhausting night, I couldn't. I couldn't do any of the things that comforted me as all of that had been engulfed in the fire that took the entire sanctuary, most of the church building, and most of my house on the afternoon of January 2, 2019.

I've always prided myself on being independent. I was raised to believe that accepting help meant weakness or that you couldn't take care of yourself. Yet, that day before, as I firmly gripped onto the arm of my parishioner he said, "You're staying with us tonight." I said, "Yeah, I might." At that point it still hadn't sunk in how little I had left.

My primary source of comfort came from the wrong place in my life: I found it in my stuff, which was now completely gone. I found comfort in my daily routines and the safe, beautiful space that was my house.

In the solace of the snow and soft sunlight that next morning, I heard the small voice that said, "I know every hair on your head and created every fiber of your being. I have got you, and I love you more than you know. I'll be with you as you step into this new light and new day." I knew in the very core of my being that God did not cause it but rather wept with me and held me tight.

Prayer: God, you are the one who knows every hair on our head, every fiber of our being, and no matter what happens, your still small voice echoes within us, that we will be more than OK. We will be whole again and are always loved more than we will ever understand. Help us breathe and rest in that. Amen.

Lynnette Cole

When the water in the skin was gone, she cast the child under one of the bushes. Then she went and sat down opposite him a good way off, about the distance of a bowshot; for she said, "Do not let me look on the death of the child." And as she sat opposite him, she lifted up her voice and wept.

—*Genesis 21:15-16 NRSV*

I have cancer," my husband said over the phone, as I sat on a bench at a beautiful retreat center. From that moment on, I knew our lives would never be the same. Although he is now in remission, the fear and doubt caused by cancer's persistence and its whispers of death continue to lurk. We all fear death. The death of a loved one, the death of a relationship, the death of our dreams. Yet, time and time again in Scripture, God shows us that God brings life out of certain death.

Hagar had made her peace with death. She had run out of water and even placed her child, Ishmael, away from her so she would not have to watch him die. She could not bear it. She offered a guttural cry to God, and God responded and saved her life and the life of her child and made of them a new nation.

I'm so thankful for all the times when God has brought life out of death. When things haven't gone the way I anticipated, God has provided patience. When the people around me haven't gotten along, God has fostered reconciliation. When people have been afraid of change, God has brought newness in the midst of death.

There have been so many times in my work in ministry when God has brought life out of death. When the Sunday sermon has not gone the way I anticipated, God provided patience from the congregation. When congregation members were unable to get along, God fostered reconciliation. When people were worried that the church would die, God brought new people to serve.

God is always bringing life out of death, but do we notice? Are we taking part in Christ's ministry of resurrection in the world? Sometimes it takes other people to point new life out to me. May you be comforted by the promise of new life if you find yourself in a season of death.

Prayer: Giver of life, when I find myself in the seasons of death, help me hold onto the promise of new life. When I am grieving, help me reach out to others who will come and grieve with me. Help me recognize that your living water is nearby, and propel me forward with the power of the Holy Spirit to receive it. Thank you for hearing my cry when I experience the death of a loved one, a relationship, or a dream. Open my eyes to the possibility of a different life, a better life, and help me help others recognize this same new life that is available to them through their faith in your son, Jesus Christ. Amen.

Jessie Squires Colwell

I went and opened for my love,
  but my love had turned, gone away.
I nearly died when he turned away.
I looked for him but couldn't find him.
  I called out to him, but he didn't answer me.

—Song of Solomon 5:6

B e brave enough to open up and love someone, and you may experience a heartbreak. Sometimes you see it coming, and you try your best to dodge it. Other times it catches you by surprise, leaving you in utter shock of its power to turn your world upside down in a single moment. No matter the how, who, or when, it always stings. It doesn't matter how many times you've been through it, it still robs you of sleep, peace, and happiness. It will piss you off, working to sow seeds of bitterness in your heart. And as much as I'd like to coddle and comfort you in this moment, because I've been here more times than I can count, that's probably not going to help. But this verse in the Song of Solomon could.

Plainly put, this woman, who'd been so madly in love, sharing erotic interlude after interlude, verse after verse in a love song for the ages, suddenly scratched the record, stops the music, and stands up in the midst of her pain and does the one thing most are scared to do: she tells her truth. "I opened my whole heart to that bastard, and they left!!! &$@#%." It has to be one of the worst feelings we can feel. When the one we sacrificed everything for, decides to leave?!! And in her case, with no warning, just packed up and left? My God. It's a blow you never forget, a hurt you always remember. And the question is, what next? How do you heal?

It's really simple. Be honest, sis. You do yourself no favors by hiding your hurt from your community, from yourself, from God. You don't need to be strong for the kids, your family, your friends, not anyone—not even yourself. People are often ready to support and pray for you, but they have to know you need them. And God desires to be with you through the worst of it, lovingly responding to your invitation.

Tell the truth about what happened and how it feels, trusting God to take it from there. The only strength you must display is vulnerability. The journey to healing starts with your honesty, with your opening up all over again. That stops the heartbreak from getting the last laugh. It clears the way for God to meet you right where it hurts, restoring you from the inside out.

Prayer: Healing God, give me the courage to open my heart and my hurt to you, to be transparent with my loved ones. Do a healing work in me that restores my joy, affirms my purpose, and empowers me for your service; in Christ's name. Amen.

Arionne Yvette Williams

∼ A Prayer for When a Loved One ∼ Dies by Suicide

God of peace, Paul claims that your peace passes understanding, that it even guards my heart (Philippians 4:7). Yet right now, I can't find peace. My heart is broken, filled with disbelief. This loss feels like a terrible nightmare. Let's be real: I will likely never fully understand why another of your dear children died by suicide. It feels too much to bear, to hold within. Remind me of your peace. Grant it, please.

God of mercy, I can't help but wonder, was this their final prayer to you? A plea for wholeness, healing? Their inner pain, relentless suffering, at times went undetected by me. How did I not see this coming? How did I not intervene? Grant me your mercy, please, so I can forgive myself and recognize only your son Jesus is our Savior.

God of forgiveness, perhaps it's my heartbreak and dismay, but I'm angry they left me here. I wasn't done living life together. And except for a select few, I can't tell anyone that while there is sadness, anger festers. People already don't know what to say, so I can't exactly answer "How are you?" with "pissed." Grant me your forgiving Spirit, that I might remember their pain and still acknowledge my own.

God of companionship, even in the most dire circumstances, situations, and events you are there. Show yourself in the coming days as I find my way to keep on living, even in the midst of my grief.

God of Eternal Life, let me find assurance that nothing can separate us from your love in life and in death. I trust my dear one is held in your arms now free from all that led to this tragedy.

God of Redemption, in the coming days, months, years—may my own heartbreak work for your good. Help me reach out to others who are suffering, to lead others in addressing the causes of suffering. Right now, God, it's just hurt I feel, but as it becomes a scar . . . give me the courage to use this part of my story to bring hope and healing to others. Amen.

Molly Simpson Hayes

*But Ruth replied, "Don't urge me to abandon you, to turn
back from following after you. Wherever you go, I will go; and
wherever you stay, I will stay. Your people will be my people, and
your God will be my God."*

—*Ruth 1:16*

One of the best sermons I ever heard was by a young man without any formal religious education or training. It had been awhile since he had stepped foot in church. Adopted by his biological grandparents, after his biological father could no longer care for him, his biological grandmother became his mother. And she had just died. He wanted to speak at her memorial service. This young man's life had never been far from trouble. He went through numerous detentions, school expulsions, depression, treatment centers, and multiple jail sentences.

What he wanted to celebrate about his mother wasn't anything you or I would showcase on social media—no fancy family vacations or picture-perfect holiday meals. Instead, he wanted to celebrate the greatest gift she gave him: unconditional love. Love even when he hurt her. Love even when he messed up. Love even when he couldn't love himself. This love had sustained him in the ditches and dumpsters he encountered. It followed him wherever he went.

This scripture from Ruth is often read as a happy, hopeful, and endearing text. It's important to realize that the context that surrounds it is hardly pleasant or happy. Everything that could go wrong has gone wrong: Naomi and her two daughters-in-law have been surrounded by poverty, famine, death, uncertainty. Great loss of every kind has been their companion.

When Naomi looks around and sees the reality of their situation, she turns to Ruth and Orpah and encourages them to leave her and go back to their own people, their own relatives. The best they can do is to leave her to find a better life—it's their only hope.

Instead, Ruth does the opposite and clings even tighter to her. Even in the worst of times, even in the face of death or despair, what's most important to Ruth is not survival. It's her loyalty and love for Naomi. It's unconditional love, a bond that remains regardless of what life throws at them.

Love that sees us through loss is a precious gift to which we can cling. It has the power to sustain us through the unimaginable and the hardest losses we face. It follows us wherever we go.

Prayer: God of love, help me be the person who offers love to others in their times of loss and despair. Help me see the sources of love and support in my own seasons of loss and hardship. May your love follow me wherever I go. Amen.

Brooke Heerwald Steiner

Then the disciples returned to their homes. But Mary stood weeping outside the tomb.

—John 20:10-11a NRSV

A fter my first miscarriage, I had overwhelming support. My church surrounded me in love, shared their own stories of loss, made me feel less isolated. My friends sent me touching cards and gifts. My sisters came over and made me and my spouse laugh, even though I didn't think laughter would ever be possible for us again. After my second miscarriage, one of my sisters curled up in bed with me, but I pushed her away. Some friends sent messages, but there was really nothing to say anyway. I withdrew in on myself. My friends and family, especially those having babies themselves, were afraid. Afraid of saying the wrong thing. Afraid of my pain. And if they weren't afraid, I pushed them away, convinced my trauma was contagious or toxic. By the time I had my third miscarriage, I didn't hear from hardly anyone. I felt so alone.

Mary Magdalene was alone that first Easter morning, or so she thought. She came to the tomb to be near her beloved teacher, even though he was dead. When she found his body gone, she ran to find other friends to help her figure out this new reality. They came, they saw, but then they went home, leaving Mary alone in her grief.

When you are faced with loss, especially compounded loss like multiple miscarriages, or losing a job right before you receive a cancer diagnosis, or going through a divorce and then losing a parent, you often feel alone and isolated. The friends who once supported you are sometimes absent, either afraid of the enormity of your grief, afraid of their own inadequacy, or dealing with their own stuff. Other times, your friends still try to support you but you push them away. If, as you face loss, you start to feel as though your community is dissipating, remember this story of Mary Magdalene in the garden, abandoned by her friends.

Because God did not abandon Mary. As she stood in the garden, bending over to look into the tomb, angels spoke to her, reminding me of the way strangers reached into my grief to offer a word of comfort when I felt completely alone. Still, in her grief, she didn't recognize them as angels, just as I didn't. And when she turned away from them, Jesus himself spoke to her. She didn't recognize him either, not until he said her name. Throughout her grief, God was there. Her eyes were opened and she could return to her friends to tell them she had seen the Lord.

Prayer: Resurrected One, open my heart to your constant presence. Remind me that I am never alone in my grief. And teach me again to reach out to others to speak of your presence. Amen.

Shannon E. Sullivan

⌒ A Prayer After a Miscarriage ⌒

God of stillness and peace,

    In this moment of searing loss, I stand before you grieving the hope of what could have been. I had a name picked out, I had picked out colors for a nursery. I had hopes and aspirations and then, all at once, cruelty stole all I had hoped. How can I go on? Open my heart to know that you are here.

Jesus, who knows the pain of death,

    In this moment, my life feels as though it is ending. The future I had planned for is no longer. I feel alienated from my spouse, my friends, and my family. I feel broken, inadequate, and alone. How can I go on? Open my mind to know that resurrection is possible.

Spirit, who breathes life,

    In this moment, I am gasping. The tears I cry are more than I can count. How can I go on? Spirit, breathe your life into my lungs, and give me the strength to endure this long dark night. Amen.

Andrea Curry

Elijah was terrified. He got up and ran for his life. He arrived at Beer-sheba in Judah and left his assistant there. He himself went farther on into the desert a day's journey. He finally sat down under a solitary broom bush. He longed for his own death: "It's more than enough, LORD! Take my life because I'm no better than my ancestors." He lay down and slept under the solitary broom bush.

—1 Kings 19:3-5a

I was a twenty-six-year-old graduate student. I was a new mom to a fourteen-day-old baby. Then three words broke everything. "You have cancer." It was the most surreal experience in the world.

Looking back, I'm certain I'd have done nearly anything for a quiet little broom bush in the wilderness to curl up under alone.

My surgery was scheduled before I left the hospital. My surgeon's discharge instructions included these words, "Take her out for some real food. She needs to eat. She's going to need her strength."

Indeed the road ahead of me was long and complicated. I would celebrate learning that I did not have cancer. Just as quickly, I would get a crash course in caring for an ileostomy. I would dry up my milk supply and put away my pump in time to trade them for drain tubes, the ostomy bag, and a catheter. I would learn how to say and spell phrases like *Ileoanal anastamosis* and *familial polyposis*.

There were so many moments along the way where the fear, the loss, and the anxiety of an uncertain future overwhelmed me. There were moments I couldn't quite bring myself to be the inspiration other people seemed to be looking for, and moments I resented them for looking to me for inspiration. Some days I wasn't even sure I could bring myself to stay awake and face more terrible daytime TV.

I could not possibly have imagined how good my life would be in ten years. I am acutely aware, even now, that the life I have wasn't a given.

It wasn't inevitable that everything would be fine. The thing that was a given, the thing that I carry with me all these years later (along with my physical scars) is that God was there with me, under my broom bush.

God sent me just what I needed to have the strength to keep going—to endure the journey that was in front of me. It showed up as a note of encouragement on my CaringBridge site, a phone call, a smile from my newborn son. It was enough. I have learned to look for those who bring a word of encouragement, a bite of sustenance, a sip of refreshment to sustain me in my wilderness ordeal, because the road ahead is long and difficult, and God will not abandon me.

Prayer: God, today I just can't. Find me in my wilderness. Give me what I need—rest, refreshment, sustenance, and encouragement—so that the journey will not be too much for me. Amen.

Amanda Baker

*Then she said to her father, "Let this one thing be done for me:
hold off for two months and let me and my friends wander the
hills in sadness, crying over the fact that I never had children."*

*"Go," he responded, and he sent her away for two months. She
and her friends walked on the hills and cried because she would
never have children.*

*When two months had passed, she returned to her father, and
he did to her what he had promised.*

—Judges 11:37-39a

During difficult times in my life and ministry, when there seemed no good solutions to the situation I am in, I've turned to my companions on the journey to help me face my loss of relationship, redefine my calling, or adjust to difficult news. Their affirmations allowed me to be brave and advocate for what I truly need. Through the encouragement of my support system, I've articulated and refined my call, which gives me the courage to make tough decisions and to endure losses head on.

Jephthah's daughter found herself in an untenable situation. Her father publicly vowed to offer God a sacrifice if he was victorious in battle. Even though Jephthah's daughter accepted her fate, I don't think she was passive and submissive. She demanded time to come to terms with her father's vow. Not only that, she required the support of her female companions. She spent two months in the hills processing with her friends what lies ahead, facing the loss of her desired future identity as a spouse and a parent.

When challenging times arise, I am grateful for the support of friends and family giving me the time and space to come to terms with new realities so I can name what is needed and to speak my piece in truth and love. The narrative from Judges inspires me to not just passively allow things to be done, but to use my agency and voice to resist oppression and injustice. Through the support of my clergy sisters, I don't have to face today alone.

When you are in an impossible situation, you are not alone. There are others who will walk the hills with you and cry.

Prayer: Help me today, O God, to treat others with grace and mercy, as they are facing losses as well. Encourage me to use my voice even when it trembles. Remind me that I am never truly alone. Amen.

Megan Stowe

～ A Prayer for the Loss ～
of a Foster Child

Loving God,
Hold me now in my grief,
as I mourn the loss of a beloved child.
Hold me in the midst of complicated emotions as I may grieve or celebrate,
feel anger or guilt, relief or confusion, or nothing at all.
May your peace that passes understanding cover me.

Be with your beloved child
when I can no longer be present in their life.
May your Spirit go ahead of them,
may they feel your love all the days of their lives,
and may the love and care they received from me
strengthen their resilience,
buffer their spirits,
and encourage continued growth.

Today and in the days to come,
grant me the space to acknowledge my loss is real,
grant me the grace to feel what I feel,
grant me listening friends, and
spare me from thoughtless comments.

And may your abounding love—
in all its height and width and depth—
cover this child,
cover those who care for this child now and into the future,
and cover me, through the power of your Holy Spirit. Amen.

Katie Lloyd

Look! I'm creating a new heaven and a new earth:
   past events won't be remembered;
   they won't come to mind.

                              —Isaiah 65:17

I once had a therapist tell me I should forget about the past and live in the present moment. Nearly quoting Disney's favorite warthog, she said, "You've got to put your past behind you." She wasn't my therapist for very long. I knew in my gut her advice was very, very wrong for me. Eventually, I got settled in with a therapist I respected and trusted. Once I felt safe, stirrings of childhood abuse, long repressed, began to drift into my consciousness.

Trauma, however blocked, has a way of making itself known. I suffered a nervous breakdown months earlier and was in treatment for a self-medicating addiction. Even though I wasn't ready to handle the weight of my past experiences, they were working hard to declare themselves, disrupting my life and unsettling my soul. Truth will out, after all.

Once that truth was out, the hard part began. The past hangs on to you. It takes hard work to disentangle yourself from it. There's no "hakuna matata"-ing your way out of trauma.

Trauma memories are literally scattered throughout your brain. When you have an experience beyond the limits of your body and brain's capacity to process, your brain can't store it normally. Instead, the memory is let loose scattershot throughout your mind, particularly affecting areas relating to speech. Some events are so traumatic, they are literally indescribable. Even so, healing from trauma usually involves telling your story over and over and over again into the soft nest of unconditional acceptance.

Thank God, then, that Christ the Logos is also Emmanuel. Christ is the Word who never leaves us. In God's presence (and usually with the help of a trusted companion such as a therapist), we can sit in the midst of these memories and know we are loved beyond measure. Shame shrivels in the light. The memories won't kill you, though it may feel like it at times. You have shown incredible strength in surviving what you did, and that strength persists. As Isaiah reminds us, God is committed to creating a new thing. The act of creating is rarely quick, easy, or necessarily enjoyable. But when God creates, God also speaks: the God who never leaves us calls you good, no matter the memories you carry.

Prayer: Ever-creating God, stay with me as I face that which ought not to be faced. Help me make sense of all that feels senseless in me and give me the words to heal my own soul. Amen.

Nancy Speas

Ashes denote that fire was.[6]

> —*Emily Dickinson*

Ashes fell on the hood of the sedan we were leaning against in the church parking lot. I'd woken up a few hours before when the phone rang. "The city's on fire," my colleague told me. I loaded up food and emergency supplies and drove across town to the church.

The administrator had already called into the radio station and announced on-air that evacuees could come to the church. When I walked in the door at five a.m., I was met by a growing crowd and the smell of bacon. I pounded a few cups of coffee and began to organize people and supplies. At the time, I didn't know that we would host more than one hundred people, many with special needs, for two weeks. I didn't know that each night I would pace the halls, wondering what would happen if the fire got closer. I didn't know that ten percent of the city would burn.

All I knew was that early on that first day of the week, I wandered outside to find our administrator leaning on the hood of a sedan in the parking lot. I offered her a cup of coffee. Her husband soon joined us, bringing eggs and bread, and as we ate, we watched the sun rise through clouds of black smoke. It was a color I hadn't seen, before or since.

Sometimes grief falls like ashes. Sometimes it consumes whole cities. On a planet facing environmental destruction, many will prophesy to such cataclysmic grief, but only hope can prevent this grief from metastasizing into despair. My hope is that in times of crisis the Spirit moves through us. The Spirit gets us out of bed, and gets us on the radio. The Spirit brings us together. The Spirit moves through our work of environmental justice, advocacy, and conservation.

The Spirit can open our eyes to God's presence at any moment; whether it is in the light breaking forth from creation or Christ made known to us in the sharing of the coffee and the breaking of the bread.

Prayer: O, Bringer of persistent beauty, make your abiding presence more known to us. Comfort us in our grief, and give us the courage to care for your creation. Amen.

Lindsey Bell-Kerr

⟋ A Prayer for When You Fear ⟍
Losing Your Child

God, I sought you in my distress. I cried out to you. You said you heard me. You said you'd be with me. This is my child. This is the child for which I prayed. This is the child that you gave me. This is the child that I held and I loved. Don't take my child. I've devoted my life to you, O Lord: loving you, worshipping you, speaking your word. I believed you when everyone around me doubted and gave up hope. I claimed your glory in the midst of everyone else's storm. And this . . . this is my child. They tell me that you are faithful and your love is steadfast and enduring. They say that you are good and that your property is to always have mercy. They say that you are trustworthy. This is my child.

I don't have the words to express how angry I am. May the Holy Spirit interpret my groans. I will not ask that your will be done. I am too afraid of your will. I do not understand your ways. I cannot comprehend your plan. I am too powerless to even save my child.

You love me like a parent loves their child—like I love my child. As I watch my child suffer and fade away, I need your love. I need your power. I need you. I cannot do this on my own.

Be the God you said you are. Be the God that heals and delivers. Be for my child the God that rescues. Be for my child like you were for Jairus's daughter. Be God for my child.

And for me, give me the strength to be mom and nurse. Give me the courage to not weep over my child's frailty. Give me the tolerance to deal with the doctors and nurses who are simply trying to do their jobs. Give me peace so that I can comfort my child.

My hope and my trust are in you. Please, please, please hear me and deliver me and my child . . . like you said you would. Amen.

Brandee Jasmine Mimitzraiem

148

Transforming Criticism

There is a thin line between criticism and constructive feedback. Criticism is often malevolence veiled in faux concern for the well-being of another. Constructive feedback on the other hand is given in the spirit of encouragement and support, helping strengthen the recipient's growing edges. Nevertheless, it takes self-awareness and emotional maturity to know the difference between the two. It also matters who is delivering the criticism or feedback, when it is delivered, and how. Regardless, no matter how aware or mature we are, some words cut deeply and can create wounds that take years to heal.

Women are often the objects of criticism. Throughout time, Scripture and science have been used to prove that women are "the lesser sex." Patriarchy has created a framework by which to judge, ridicule, and devalue women, especially women leaders. We see this in backhanded compliments, anonymous complaints, and comments focused on our appearance. This criticism is used to distract and discourage, and sometimes these tactics work. Other times, criticism propels us forward to lead in more authentic ways that empower us to make bold moves and face new challenges with a greater sense of self-confidence.

In these devotions, you will find women who transform criticism by centering their faith in God. God is indeed on the side of the brokenhearted, those who weep, and the heavy laden. These women use Scripture to push back against the criticizers and naysayers, but more importantly, to construct a new narrative of affirmation. The devotions on the following pages are grounded in Scripture, covered in prayer, and are unapologetically transformative.

Theresa S. Thames

Shout loudly; don't hold back;
* raise your voice like a trumpet!*
Announce to my people their crime,
* to the house of Jacob their sins.*
                    —Isaiah 58:1

"You're too loud."
    "You talk too much."
  "Slow down. I can't understand you."

These are all things I have been told throughout my time in leadership. They are also all true statements. I didn't realize how much these words were affecting me, however, until I commented to my spiritual director one day that I felt like I was stuffing everything that I felt called to say deep down inside of me.

I was aware that I was tempering my voice in certain settings because I thought that was who I was supposed to be. As people were telling me that I was too loud, too outspoken, I took this as a rebuke to be silent. I started to believe the lie that it was better if I just didn't speak at all.

But then the words, stories, and opinions born out of my experience were completely missing. When I silence myself in order to be who other people expect, I am not being faithful to who God has called me to be.

Does that mean I can say whatever I want all the time? Certainly not. But it also means that I do not need to silence myself. God created me to be a person who is outspoken, with a loud laugh that echoes through crowds, who sometimes gets so excited that I talk too fast. My voice honors who I am uniquely created to be.

The prophet Isaiah was called to name injustices loudly, raising his voice like a trumpet. In the same way, I am being unfaithful when I see injustice and don't speak out against it. I am not being true to my calling when I give up my voice in order to appease others with what they want to hear. Using my voice is an act of resistance.

It's time for faithful Christians to raise our voices like the trumpet sound. It's time to shout and not hold back. It's time to claim our voices to speak against the injustices in our world.

Prayer: Lord of life, you have given me my voice, my call, and my story for a reason. Empower me to use these gifts faithfully in this world for your honor and glory. Amen.

Michelle Bodle

Calling the Twelve to him, he began to send them out two by two and gave them authority over impure spirits. These were his instructions: "Take nothing for the journey except a staff—no bread, no bag, no money in your belts. Wear sandals but not an extra shirt. Whenever you enter a house, stay there until you leave that town. And if any place will not welcome you or listen to you, leave that place and shake the dust off your feet as a testimony against them." They went out and preached that people should repent. They drove out many demons and anointed many sick people with oil and healed them.

—Mark 6:7-13 NIV

D ust has always been part of my life. I grew up surrounded by wheat fields, the air thick with the smell of red dirt. The rhythm of my family life, even now when many of us have other careers, is rooted in the seasons of the earth. Fall is for planting, winter for dormancy, spring for growing, and summer for harvesting. Harvest is the biggest event of the year. It's chaotic, dangerous, and beautiful all at the same time.

On those long summer days in the field, there are days in which everything goes according to plan. It's sunny, but not humid. There's a breeze, but not a gale. Everyone shows up where they are supposed to. All the moving pieces work in harmony without breaking down. That's a perfect harvest day.

Then, there are the days that try every fiber of my patience. If I am frustrated, that means that everyone else is too, because their roles are greater and more stressful than mine. Those are the days when the field is too muddy to run the combine without stopping to have a tractor pull it out of the muck, or when all we seem to do is put out fires, sometimes literal ones. Everything breaks down and nothing is running.

Those days are the worst.

No matter which kind of day I have had in the field with my family, the best part of the day is the shower at night. I generally have dirt in places that I didn't know exist. It is a wonderful feeling to stand in the water and to watch that dirt swirl down the drain. Washing off the dust has become an important practice in my life.

When Jesus sent out the twelve, he gave them very specific instructions on what to take and how to respond when they came to a place in which their message and presence was not well received. Shake off the dust and move on. This has become the way I deal with criticism. Shaking off the dust doesn't mean that it didn't exist. It doesn't mean that those dusty days didn't change my heart or make me weary. It doesn't mean that those who provided the dust were right or fair or loving. It does mean that I get to control how I respond to actions and words that I have no control over. Shaking off the dust of the day gives me the courage that I need to wake up and do it all again.

Prayer: God of the harvest, the crops are plentiful, but the laborers are few. Help me shake off the dust so that I can continue serving you. Amen.

Shannon Rodenberg

*Adopt the attitude that was in Christ Jesus: Though he was
in the form of God, he did not consider being equal with God
something to exploit. But he emptied himself by taking the form
of a slave and by becoming like human beings.*

—Philippians 2:5-7a

Sorry, we don't think you're ready for this." These are words that no
one wants to hear. As a young woman, called to a traditionally male
profession, these words carry a heavy weight, and I heard them from my
credentialing board when I went before them the first time.

These words of criticism were words of imprisonment. These were words
that I needed to transform into something life-giving. My vocation is a call
from God, not from any board. This call has been affirmed time and time
again in my own devotional life and from trusted family, friends, mentors,
and teachers. How could one group of people do so much damage? As it
turned out, neither myself nor God would let this be the final word.

I grieved my expectation for job advancement. I grieved for the work
that I had done and now would have to redo in the future. Out of that
grief, I sought help. I reached out to a colleague who also received a similar
response from the board. I reached out to people who were gifted writers
and former board members who could help me prepare for the future in-
terviews. I embraced the love that I received and in turn wanted to share
that love.

Paul says, "Adopt the attitude of Jesus." Empty yourself of the restric-
tive, damaging language and be filled with words of love and life. The
mind of Jesus paints a beautiful picture of love that dictates life, love for
God, and love of neighbor. When I realized my vocation didn't have to
be shaped by someone's perception of my mistakes or faults, I was able to
transform the criticism I received into acknowledgment that we are all
human and that we are all created for great things. My great thing is being
faithful to my calling and not letting anyone convince me otherwise.

Prayer: God, I pray today for all who are hearing criticism and internalizing it, causing further harm. When I hear criticism, enable me to hear it, grieve for what could have been, and then defiantly embrace the life you have called me to anyway. May my great thing in this life honor you. Amen.

Catherine Christman

∼ A Prayer of Discernment ∼
After Receiving Critique

God of the critics and the critiqued, thank you for the hard conversations. Even in my anger, disappointment, and stomach-ache-inducing hurt feelings, I know you're with me. Send your Holy Spirit to give me a new way of seeing things, and remind me that every confrontation is still connection and opportunity for seeing you in a new way. Don't let me quit when things get tough, and don't let me fall for the lies that say I should be a nice, quiet Christian woman. Instead, remind me of all those who got things done because they were more committed to your vision of justice than they were to pleasing people. Show me how to be as wise as a snake and to lead fearlessly. Amen.

Violet Johnicker

∼ A Prayer Before Entering ∼
a Contentious Meeting

Holy God, you know my mind and heart. You know my worries and anxieties. You know my hopes and goals for this meeting. Go before me, Lord. Prepare the way. Open minds. Soften hearts. Help us treat each other in the way that we wish to be treated. Help us to truly listen to each other. Help us seek you and your will in this meeting above our own human agendas. I lift up this meeting and its outcomes to you; in the power of Jesus's name I pray. Amen.

Sara M. Nelson

Weeping may stay all night,
*   but by morning, joy!*
                            —Psalm 30:5b

I have cried a lot of tears in my life. It has taken me a long time to not see this as a liability because of all the messages I have heard about emotions being a sign of weakness. And more than that, a weak female thing. I never wanted to be weak. I never wanted to seem weak.

There are times when people let me down. There are times when an entire group of people let me down. There are times when my family lets me down. There are times when I let myself down. And there are times when I let other people down.

When we hear people's criticism of us, we first have to figure out if that criticism is deserved, and if it is, what we are going to do with it. We get to choose if we will accept it or reject it, and in what way. And when we hear criticism, deserved or not, we have to decide how to react. Crying is not a sign of weakness. Feeling deeply that you have let other people down or made a misstep and regret it is not a sign of weakness. For far too long, emotions have been cast as weak. Women have been told to "toughen up" in order to be taken seriously. Nope. Women need not be anything other than who we are. If you want to cry when someone criticizes you, then do so. If you do not want to cry, then don't. Do what your heart needs to do.

This verse promises that whatever emotion we have in response to letting people down, it will not last forever. We may weep all night long—or rage all night long—but by morning, there will be joy. Sometimes this joy is hard won, but it is assured. No one gets to steal your joy forever, but only for a night—no matter how deserved the criticism is. And if the criticism is undeserved, then make that night the shortest of the year.

Prayer: God of grace, give me the wisdom to know how to respond to criticism I receive. If I need to accept that I have done something wrong, give me the strength to do so and the ability to make needed changes. If I need to let all that go, help me do just that. In either case, enable me to feel my emotions fully and see them as signs of humanity and strength. And then, O God, turn those emotions into joy. Amen.

Emily A. Peck-McClain

Then Jesus began to teach his disciples: "The Human One must
suffer many things and be rejected by the elders, chief priests,
and the legal experts, and be killed, and then, after three days,
rise from the dead." He said this plainly. But Peter took hold of
Jesus and, scolding him, began to correct him. Jesus turned and
looked at his disciples, then sternly corrected Peter: "Get behind
me, Satan. You are not thinking God's thoughts but human
thoughts."

—Mark 8:31-33

Square your hips!" "Point your toes!" The corrections barked by my ballet teacher startled me, but I quickly tried to take them into account and responded to the critique with "Thank you." I was taught that when the teacher gave me corrections this was a good thing—it meant she thought I had potential; it meant he thought I had the capacity to improve. Conversely, I was also taught that when I no longer received critiques from a teacher that it was a bad thing—it meant she thought I was hopeless; it meant he thought I was no longer worth his time. In the dance world, I learned to take criticism, incorporate what was helpful into my practice, and be grateful someone cared enough to correct me.

When I entered the professional world, I forgot this lesson. "You need to do more for the youth!" "You need to recruit more volunteers!" The words that came from others felt less like gentle corrections aimed at my improvement, and more like hurtful barbs aimed at telling me that I was no good, that I didn't deserve to be their leader.

When Jesus begins to teach the disciples about what must happen to him, about his suffering, death, and resurrection, Peter scolds Jesus. Jesus, in turn, sternly corrects Peter, saying to him, "Get behind me, Satan!" I can imagine that to Peter, that felt like a hurtful barb aimed at telling him he was no good, that he didn't deserve to be a disciple. And yet, we know that Jesus loved Peter, saw potential in him, and knew Peter had the capacity to improve. Later in Scripture, Jesus calls Peter a name again, but this time he names Peter his rock, the foundation on which the church will be built.

There are times in my life when I need to look at the criticism I receive and discern—is this aimed to help or to hurt? Does it feel like hurt but is actually helpful? If I can find a way to look at the person offering the critique and say "Thank you," perhaps I can transform any criticism I receive. Thank you for having faith in my potential. Thank you for believing that I have the capacity to improve. I can then take the criticism, incorporate what is helpful into my practice, and be grateful someone cares enough to correct me, just like Jesus did with Peter.

Prayer: Teaching God, thank you for giving me the capacity to improve. Help me see my own potential, and to give thanks for those who help point the way, even if it doesn't feel so great at the time. Amen.

Bethany Willers

Forgive us our sins, for we also forgive everyone who has wronged us. And don't lead us into temptation.

—*Luke 11:4*

As a woman, there is greater expectation to readily forgive others of their unhelpful criticism. The reason being that it is not "attractive" for a woman to become frustrated and angry. I readily admit that I've addressed inappropriate comments using phrases such as "it seems like . . .," "I think it might be . . .," and other relatively passive qualifiers to statements in which I ultimately address the inappropriate comment made to me. Have grace! I am a work in progress like the rest of us, and the truth is, it is scary.

I do not lift up forgiveness as a way to condone nor ignore accountability—this is the imperative women are often given by others who are uncomfortable with frustration. Justice is important. Being a voice for what is just means I value my voice and add it to the chorus of women who do not consent to undue comments or criticism.

I lift up forgiveness as a means by which I release those who wrong me from the power I give them when I choose to hold onto the pain from that wrong. Forgiveness is an act of resistance: to reclaim authority over my own narrative, instead of letting it be dictated by the criticism of others. Forgiveness means reclaiming my power and my story despite the attempt of others to harm. Forgiveness means letting go of the pain, mistrust, and anger I choose to harbor in me when I give others power. Instead, I choose to let those things in me pass away and die, in order for me to gain a new way of being in the world quite apart from what has festered due to others.

Transformed by that death, I live into a narrative of resurrection. I choose to give voice to a resurrection narrative that calls me to speak boldly with authority and vulnerability to a greater purpose—a vision of God that is not dictated by others' criticism of me. What of others do you need to let die in you so that you can choose your own resurrection narrative?

Prayer: Loving God, forgive me for the ways my pain can do harm to others just as I easily give power to pain and harm. The temptation to righteously cling to the harm others inflict on me can feel so great, but I persist in your power that living life as resurrected people calls to me louder. Sustain me in your love with each moment I speak out truth in justice. Persist with me in the journey to boldly live out my own vulnerability, truth, and power as a woman in religious leadership. Amen.

Kendall Kridner-Protzmann

⌒ **Another Kind of Serenity Prayer** ⌒

O God, grant me the wisdom to know when to hit delete and when to pause and listen.

When the criticism spewing from my computer screen is purely spiteful, reflecting the deep unhealth of the sender, grant me the serenity to take a deep breath, pray for my critic, and press delete. As I do so, I ask that you delete the power of its negativity to linger in my mind. Remind me to accept that I cannot change those who criticize me.

But God, when the criticism on my screen is valid, open my heart to hear it. When it challenges my privilege, help me not to hit delete but to seek to understand and transform. Give me courage to swallow my pride and take down my defenses. May listening change me into the disciple you have called me to be.

O God, grant me the wisdom to know when to hit delete and when to pause and listen. Amen.

Shannon E. Sullivan

*Your servant is here among the people you have chosen, a great
people, too numerous to count or number. So give your servant a discerning heart to govern your people and to distinguish between right
and wrong. For who is able to govern this great people of yours?*

—1 Kings 3:8-9 NIV

I listened intently, a smile plastered to my face, and nodded at what I deemed appropriate times. "And another thing . . ." the man continued, beginning yet another barrage of criticism. I was sitting in my annual
review. Unfortunately, the committee of nine was only three strong this
evening, with one of those being someone who had hardly interacted with
me in the past year. He greeted me with a smile as I came in and said,
"Well, the good news is we don't want to fire you, but we did have a few
concerns." The "we" was what my mama taught me is "the royal we," and
it really meant him.

I am a well-trained southern woman who knows that a closed mouth
and pleasant smile go a long way in avoiding awkward social situations
in which I could be erroneously pegged as confrontational, abrasive, or
uncooperative. In other words, the "b-word," which in this case did not
stand for boss. But, something internally clicked for me in that moment. I
realized that while I may not feel I owe it to myself to defend my integrity
and my work, I would never have let someone sling such false accusations
at any other person without saying something. I owed it to the truth that
my work and integrity could stand on their own without requiring such
submissive passivity.

I met the challenge head-on and objectively addressed his concerns one
by one. I remained calm, stuck to the facts, listened carefully to hear both
what was said and unsaid, and offered correction to misconceptions. The
other two attendees remained silent, only calling the following day to apologize for their colleague's aggressiveness, assuring me that they didn't share
his concerns.

Sometimes silence does more harm than good. Sometimes you won't earn the respect of others no matter what you do. Sometimes it really isn't your fault and people's perceptions are simply out of your hands. In those cases, pan for the gold of constructive criticism. When you sift it out, some pans will yield more treasure than others. Keep sifting, holding onto what's helpful and let the rest flow downstream.

Prayer: Lord, give me a discerning heart as I lead. Help me speak truth. For others, for myself, and for your sake. Amen.

Nicole de Castrique Jones

"Ask, and you will receive. Search, and you will find. Knock, and the door will be opened to you. For everyone who asks, receives. Whoever seeks, finds. And to everyone who knocks, the door is opened."

—*Matthew 7:7-8*

As my peers celebrated their accomplishments, most of us having spent at least nine years to reach this final point of professional credentialing, I received my feedback: "not this year." I was offered some explanation of needing a bit more emotional maturity and healing. While not the intention, it felt like it was somehow my fault that my parents divorced, my brother died by suicide, and my husband left before my twenty-fifth birthday. Life happens and there are circumstances that are out of our control.

As I waited for the next year's credentialing process and prepared again, it was a different reason but the same words: "not this year." My response went from crocodile tears to anger. I was the senior leader. It didn't make sense. I had felt God calling me to this work since I was fifteen years old. I had resisted, prayed, resisted, agreed, and asked for the stamina, courage, and strength needed. Had I failed? Had I misheard God?

When my devotional text the next day was these words from Matthew, I rolled my eyes and uttered a choice expletive in the (not so) holiest of prayers. Yet, by the end of the week I felt the Holy Spirit's comfort. I heard her saying: keep knocking, you've been waiting for the wrong people to open the door.

Whether it's being passed over for a promotion, a new job, a leadership position, or receiving a failing grade in a subject we love, we live in a world of feedback. Workplace evaluations are part of our annual calendar and it's all exhausting. So, how is it we respond when the criticism burdens us?

Without my own professional setbacks, I likely would not have married my incredible partner, enjoyed many of the career opportunities I have, or grown into who God created me to be. Ultimately, I approached what became my last credentialing interview in peace.

What if we're relying on the people of this world as opposed to the One who created it and us? What if we can't even see the door that God is opening? What if our dreams for ourselves are much smaller than God's dreams for us? What dream does God have for us once the hurt and criticism wane?

Prayer: God, grant the tenacity to overcome criticism and the wisdom to hear your voice in it while ignoring the unwarranted. Help me rely on you in times of uncertainty and trust that your dreams for me are even greater than my own. Amen.

Molly Simpson Hayes

*"Please, my master, pay no attention to this despicable man
Nabal. He's exactly what his name says he is! His name means
fool, and he is foolish! But I myself, your servant, didn't see the
young men that you, my master, sent. I pledge, my master, as
surely as the Lord lives and as you live, that the Lord has held
you back from bloodshed and taking vengeance into your own
hands! But now let your enemies and those who seek to harm my
master be exactly like Nabal!"*

—1 Samuel 25:25-26

Abigail is a fierce woman. She's intelligent and politically savvy. And she's surrounded by dangerous immaturity. Her husband, Nabal, and the anointed-but-on-the-run King David are dancing dangerously with each other, each more concerned with protecting his own ego than the well-being of others (not that we've ever seen that before).

So when she hears of Nabal's dismissiveness and David's power-hungry, potentially violent reaction brewing, she breaks the cycle of posturing between the men. Abigail not only brings food to men hungry for war but also reminds David that vengeance, especially for the sake of reputation, should not be the characterization of "the man after God's own heart."

Nabal was a fool, desperate to prove his strength by ignoring the help he'd received. David was about to act a fool, desperate to prove his strength in the deadliest of ways. Abigail, on the other hand, saw these two men for what they were—insecure. Put in First Lady Michelle Obama's words, "bullies [are] just scared people hiding inside scary people."[1] An over-the-top show of strength will ultimately impress nobody. It certainly doesn't change how God sees you—or them.

So the next time someone lobs a comment your way, ask yourself, *Is this comment a perspective I value? Does this person care about my well-being, or does the comment say more about them than it does about me?* If it does, don't be compelled to respond for their sake. Let it go.

Personal attacks are not constructive criticism. Personal attacks are mirrors into the soul of the speaker. And while snapping back or beating yourself up may initially seem like sensible responses, they do not reflect the truth of who you are—a child of God, gifted and called in specific ways to live in this broken and beautiful world. If criticism does not come from a place of knowing your worth and potential, let it go. God knows who you are, and you have nothing to prove.

Prayer: Discerning God, you who know me at my worst and at my best. Grant me the wisdom to discern the comments worth holding onto and the ones I can let go. I want to be good, God, but sometimes your children say things that cut deeper than I'd like to bear. And when those people are unbearable, O God—and you know who I'm talking about—help me see their attacks for what they are: mirrors into their own soul. Even from the depth of my pain, O God—because these attacks HURT—help me respond with empathy and compassion over cheap vengeance; in Jesus's compassionate name I pray. Amen.

Allie Scott

~ **A Prayer for the Misunderstood** ~

God of the ebbing and flowing moon, just as you created the universe in all its expansiveness and complexity, so you created me in all my expansiveness and complexity. You know my body and my heart. You know my desires. You know my orientation and my identity.

There are others who do not understand me. They label me and try to put me in a box that doesn't fit. They tell me that I'm just "in a phase," that someday I will emerge and be just like them. But your Queer Spirit lifts me beyond the norms of society and delights in my extraordinary being.

God of radiance, help me be more like the moon, who winks at me with her phases as she dances through cycles of shadows and light. Remind me to glance up when the moon is full and as she basks in her true form. May I be like the full moon, O God, and may my "phases" lead me to come out of the shadows and shine my truest light. Amen.

Laurel A. Capesius

I lift up my eyes to the hills—
    from where will my help come?
My help comes from the LORD,
    who made heaven and earth.

He will not let your foot be moved;
    he who keeps you will not slumber.
He who keeps Israel
    will neither slumber nor sleep.

The LORD is your keeper;
    the LORD is your shade at your right hand.
The sun shall not strike you by day,
    nor the moon by night.

The LORD will keep you from all evil;
    he will keep your life.
The LORD will keep
    your going out and your coming in
    from this time on and forevermore.

—Psalm 121 NRSV

Like many others, I keep a collection of encouraging notes, cards, and the like from people who send me these things. I take the notes out of the box to read when I have a hard day or week. They are treasures. The other notes go in the trash. You know the ones. Usually anonymous, but sometimes bold enough to be claimed, these messages are ones of criticism and likely full of projection and self-doubt on the writer's part. Lately, I have found myself wondering if I should keep these kinds of notes too. They are a part of my journey, after all.

The ancient Hebrew people sang this psalm as they were journeying to a holy place, and they knew that the journey would have low places that would leave them wondering where God was in all of this. The notes that get thrown in the trash are my lowest places and have absolutely made me wonder where God was. The valleys are part of my journey.

The criticism is part of our story. Every time I have received one of these notes, God has helped me figure out if there was truth in the criticism, because there might be something I can learn. In those cases, I can move past the writer's refusal to approach me directly and receive assurance from God that their words will now be used for good.

Perhaps the lesson is that if we discard criticism like these notes too quickly, we just might miss an opportunity for God to break in and lead us somewhere surprising.

Prayer: Dear God, help me sit long enough with uncomfortable criticism so that I can sort out if there is some truth in it. Keep me journeying with you as I grow. Assure me that you are my help. Amen.

Emily L. Stirewalt

"Look, I'm sending you as sheep among wolves. Therefore, be wise as snakes and innocent as doves. Watch out for people—because they will hand you over to councils and they will beat you in their synagogues. They will haul you in front of governors and even kings because of me so that you may give your testimony to them and to the Gentiles. Whenever they hand you over, don't worry about how to speak or what you will say, because what you can say will be given to you at that moment. . . . Don't think that I've come to bring peace to the earth. I haven't come to bring peace but a sword."

—Matthew 10:16-19, 34

Overpromising is as old as time, but Jesus wasn't about that life. He offered no quick fixes, shortcuts, or easy outs. Instead, he straight up said that preaching the real good news of God's love for justice was going to result in a lot of disagreement, public criticism, and fights. Given that pretty terrible sales pitch for being a disciple, who's going to say, "Yes, send me!"? You did. I did. Our ancestors in the faith did, and our heroes of today do. We keep saying yes, every day, even and especially when things get hard, because Jesus told us we could expect that reaction from folks.

I have a weekly column in our local newspaper where I write about politics and religion and, as you might imagine, not everyone agrees with the perspectives of a young, progressive, female Christian leader. I've gotten some pretty intense e-mails and letters from people telling me that I'm doing more harm than good, that I have a poison pen, and that I shouldn't call myself a Christian. The first few months I was writing, I dreaded the day my columns would be published because I knew I'd have some demoralizing e-mails waiting for me when I opened my inbox.

It's times like that when this passage really speaks to me. Jesus knew it wasn't going to be easy for those of us who proclaim God's radically inclusive love and call for things to be the way God wants. So, I keep writing back to everyone who writes to me, and I invite them out for conversation and coffee. I keep writing what the Spirit speaks to me even when I know everyone won't agree. I take comfort in knowing that Jesus's invitation wasn't for me to be nice and nonconfrontational, but rather to be ready for the fight.

Prayer: Lord who created me to be snakelike, thank you for all the gifts you've blessed me with. Show me how to use them to serve you in unexpected ways and to be prepared for the challenges Jesus promised me we'd face. Amen.

Violet Johnicker

Fools see their own way as right,
   but the wise listen to advice.
Fools reveal their anger right away,
   but the shrewd hide their contempt.
Those who state the truth speak justly,
   but a false witness deceives.
Some chatter on like a stabbing sword,
   but a wise tongue heals.
Truthful lips endure forever,
   but a lying tongue lasts only for a moment.
Deceit is in the heart of those who plan evil,
   but there is joy for those who advise peace.
No harm happens to the righteous,
   but the wicked receive their fill of trouble.
The LORD detests false lips;
   he favors those who do what is true.

—Proverbs 12:15-22

I nervously picked up the phone as I saw my new supervisor's name on the caller ID. "Hi Jen, I received a call from a stakeholder who has concerns about you. Is there anything I should know before I return his call?" This particular stakeholder and I had never been on the same page. I wasn't surprised to hear he was unhappy, though I assured my supervisor it was nothing worth him getting a call.

A few days later, I asked how their meeting went. My supervisor summarized their conversation with one comment: "Ultimately, I think his problems are less about your leadership and more about the fact that you can wear skirts instead of just pants."

I immediately laughed at this comment—both because of the way it was phrased and as a release of tension I had allowed to build up. I previously suspected the critiques I received from this man were related to my gender, but hearing it named by a male colleague was more freeing than I expected it to be. It was refreshing to hear a male supervisor call this what it was: sexism.

Here's the thing about serving as a woman in leadership: men and women alike critique everything about women leaders. These critiques include what we wear, how we speak, the shape of our bodies, the length of our hair. Women leaders are expected to smile more, be polite, and apologize often.

I'm done apologizing. I am not sorry for being a woman.

No matter what we face or what critiques we receive, I am sure that no criticism of my personhood—of my gender—is ever worth listening to. No critique of my leadership based on my being a woman is worthy of being heard.

God came into this world by a woman. Jesus entrusted the good news of his resurrection to women. God has called me, and you, to faithfully use our gifts to live into our passions, whether that is in the academy, board room, church, or surgical wing.

Plenty of people work against this, but Proverbs tells us, "Fools see their own way as right," and I will no longer listen to the foolish who refuse to see the light of God within me. As women, we must speak and live our truth that God has created and equipped us to lead.

Prayer: God of truth, thank you for the gift of being a woman, and the gift of wearing both skirts and pants. This day and every day, help me fight the patriarchy that stands in the way of the life you have called me to, and lead me to find the fullness of joy that is found in your peace. Amen.

Jen Tyler

A Prayer for Imposter Syndrome

God, it feels so good when others think I know what I'm doing. But, Lord, you see the terror I feel underneath the facade of competence, like a duck gliding across still waters, hoping no one notices how hard I'm paddling just below the surface.

Who am I to lead other people when I can barely lead myself well?

I want to believe that I am made in your image. But, you're the Great I Am. I am not. My image of what it is to be holy always makes me feel like my heart is miles away from true holiness.

Jesus, why can't I actually have the spiritual life that other people think I have?

I'm tempted to pray for the strength to grow into the person I think I should be so that I'd meet my own expectations. But, God, I know that it would never feel like enough, and the finish line would keep moving.

I'm tempted to pray for you to help me accept myself as "enough," just as I am. I know you already love me exactly as I am. And I know that because you love me, you desire more for me and my life.

So all I can pray for in this moment is that you deliver me from these temptations. Help me see with your eyes for just a moment. Give me the courage to step past all of these false versions of myself, avoiding the shame trying to nip at my ankles.

Holy Spirit, fill me with your healing and sustaining power so that I will be ready to step out into this world as my true self.

And, God, give me some compassion for when one of those imposters shows up again—they're trying to help and to protect me. But I trust that you are protection enough for my true self and that you need the real me to show up in this world. Amen.

Sarah Harrison-McQueen

I thought, I'll forget him;
   I'll no longer speak in his name.
But there's an intense fire in my heart,
   trapped in my bones.
   I'm drained trying to contain it;
      I'm unable to do it.

—*Jeremiah 20:9*

This is the verse that caused me to "come out" in the middle of my seminary studies. A classmate preached on it during a perfectly ordinary Wednesday night chapel service, and while they spoke about the importance of sharing the gospel, these words pierced me for a different reason.

I had been containing the immensity of my truth for several months, afraid of what would happen if I revealed it. I had arrived at seminary with a plan to get ordained. I knew that if I came out, that plan would be ruined by church polity: "Self-avowed practicing homosexuals are not to be certified as candidates, ordained as ministers, or appointed to serve in The United Methodist Church."[2] Those words scratched at my soul like sandpaper the moment I realized I was not straight, filling me simultaneously with hot fury and paralyzing fear.

My own truth about how God created me became a fire shut up in my bones, threatening to incinerate me from within. I became weary with holding it in, and eventually, I could not. I called a friend over to my apartment and collapsed in tears of relief as I forced the words out of my chest in front of another person for the first time: "I'm gay."

My spiritual life immediately changed. The fire was no longer shut up in my bones. I had set it free in the world for others to see, a terrifying and liberating experience.

At some point, you will find yourself in a place where there is a fire shut up in your bones. You become weary of your own silence. You become weary of containing your righteous anger. You become weary of your grief, your loneliness, your pain. There is a fire within you that you must bravely let loose in the world.

Prayer: Divine Fire, threaten me with your heat. Remind me of the deep truth I hold in my bones. Cause me to wonder why I feel the need to contain it. Grant me the courage to let the fire loose. Grant me the courage to blaze as a beacon in a world in need of more Light. Amen.

Kai Carico

*Is this the kind of fast I choose, a day of self-affliction, of
bending one's head like a reed and of lying down in mourning
clothing and ashes? Is this what you call a fast, a day acceptable to the LORD? Isn't this the fast I choose: releasing wicked
restraints, untying the ropes of a yoke, setting free the mistreated,
and breaking every yoke?*

—Isaiah 58:5-6

L et's get rid of forty bags in forty days," I promoted. "We have too much
stuff. Time to clean it out!" In our predominately upper-class church,
this was largely true. So, we joined the #40Bagsin40Days challenge. Our
Lenten discipline would fill jumbo-sized trash bags, small plastic bags,
donation bags for Goodwill, and recycling bags.

Almost as an afterthought, we also gave out small paper bags, and invited people to get rid of their emotional baggage. Anyone with spiritual
wounds, long-lasting grudges, or painful pasts could write down that emotional junk, and place it in the paper bag for Lent.

In my mind, those emotional bags were a concession to people who
didn't want to make a physical sacrifice. This Lenten adventure was to
clean out our literal closets. Fasting from possessions would make this day
acceptable to the Lord!

Then, I got the e-mail. You know the kind, the vindictive attack that
takes your breath away. When I read it on the morning of Ash Wednesday,
I felt like a bruised reed about to break. I couldn't concentrate on anything
besides the emotional attack. I was angry, bitter, and hurt. I wanted to lash
out and run away.

As worship started, I noticed that the person who wrote the e-mail sat in
the pews and glowered at me. I bowed my head and prayed.

After the service, I printed out the e-mail. I read through it one more
time. I cried. Then I put the criticism in the paper bag and stapled it shut.
And I kept that "Emotional Baggage" bag on my shelf throughout all of

Lent. Each time my mind brought up the criticism, I would turn toward the bag and whisper, "It's over there. I can pick it back up at the end of Lent." Thus, for forty days, I gave the pain to God. This was not the fast I chose, but this was the fast that chose me. I did not achieve my goal of getting rid of forty bags of physical stuff. Instead, my judgmental and wounded soul was cleansed.

Several months after Easter, I recycled the bag without opening it. I was no longer tied to the criticism. God had released me. I had been set free.

Prayer: God, when I am bent down, raise me up. When I am yoked to trouble, release me. When I am cast out, accept me. Free me so that I can set others free too. Amen.

Diane M. Kenaston

*He said, "In a certain city there was a judge who neither feared
God nor respected people. In that city there was a widow who
kept coming to him, asking, 'Give me justice in this case against
my adversary.' For a while he refused but finally said to himself,
I don't fear God or respect people, but I will give this widow
justice because she keeps bothering me. Otherwise, there will be no
end to her coming here and embarrassing me." The Lord said,
"Listen to what the unjust judge says. Won't God provide justice
to his chosen people who cry out to him day and night? Will he
be slow to help them? I tell you, he will give them justice quickly.
But when the Human One comes, will he find faithfulness on
earth?"*

—Luke 18:2-8

There are few things that infuriate me more than an unjust judge. With a spouse in the legal field, I find that many of our conversations turn to the courts and what the unjust judges among us are saying these days. Just like the ruling of the unjust judge in this scripture, even a seemingly positive decision can be laced with rationale that doesn't embody the ideals of justice. I'm left wondering how much it matters that the unjust judge rules in favor of the widow, only because he's bothered, if at the end of the day he still gives the widow justice.

It matters because he didn't just give her this ruling. She demanded it. The widow is my hero, for in her courage and determination I see the woman I aspire to be. She does not stand down in the face of unjust authority. She does not try a quieter or more socially acceptable approach. She instead remains true to her convictions and demands she be heard.

Unjust judges are not solely in the courts. They swarm businesses, family reunions, and social media platforms with their toxicity and their dismissal of human rights. In the face of unjust judges, I turn to God embodied in a woman risking everything for the sake of what is owed to her. I turn to God embodied in the voices of the marginalized—Womanist, Indigenous, Latinx, and Queer voices, to name a few. I turn to God embodied in those who have dismissed the judgments wrongfully pronounced on their being and have demanded that they be seen and honored.

God will give justice quickly, Jesus says. Indeed, God has always been on the side of those who have been oppressed, and now Jesus asks of our faithfulness. I must ask myself: *Am I faithful to the God of justice and liberation, and am I doing the work within myself and out in the world so that my answer can be a resounding yes?*

Prayer: God of Justice, help me recognize and address injustice in the world, and help me be open to receiving criticism from those who experience marginalization in ways I may not see and may even cause. Fuel my courage and my determination that I may join in the work of liberation for all your people. Amen.

Laurel A. Capesius

A Prayer for When Someone Judges Your Body Instead of Your Body of Work

O God, not again. Not those piercing words, "You're good at this, but . . . I worry about your weight" or some other equally offensive critique of my body offered under the veil of, "I just say it because I care." As if those words are a license to speak about my body, or the way I dress, or how I fix my hair, or the fact that I despise pantyhose under the guise of "caring."

I am so sick of being judged on my physical body instead of my body of work. I am capable and smart and kind and loving and caring and good at what I do. Why can't that be what takes center stage? Over and over these jabs make me want to scream.

You listen to my frustrated cries, my wailing that I'm not good enough. And you patiently wait to shout back at me that I am enough. Now, as I am. As you made me. God, honestly, I'm so tired of trying to defend this body that you created and called good, the body that I've struggled to accept as beautiful despite the things I wish I could change.

I can take back my power, because I am strong, and this is wrong.

God, grant me the indignation to say boldly, "You know what? This is NOT OK. You do NOT get to say whatever you want about my body. It's mine. Back off and make a different choice the next time you think you can offer some 'caring' advice about a body that is not your own."

God, give me the courage to take back my image and claim my body as my own vessel of courage, wisdom, and beauty. Restore my spirit to walk tall as I walk humbly with you. Make it so, God. Make it so. Amen.

Shannon Rodenberg

"Don't judge, so that you won't be judged. You'll receive the same judgment you give. Whatever you deal out will be dealt out to you."

—*Matthew 7:1-2*

The feeling of panic started in my gut, but it quickly worked its way to my heart, causing it to beat louder and faster. Then it moved from my heart to my eyes, causing them to well with hot, angry tears. It worked its way to my knees until they felt like they could not, would not, bear my weight. How was I supposed to keep doing my job?

In the middle of work, a well-seasoned, well-respected man practically shouted at me, "When are you going to stop with this Mickey Mouse teaching?"

I could not be sure if he was calling me or the topic "Mickey Mouse," but either way, it did not feel good. It felt like an assault in the middle of my presentation, unfairly harsh, unapologetically critical. All of my impulses invited me to respond in the same harsh, critical vein, to give back to him a little of what he was giving me.

This is completely natural. Behavioral scientists call it complementary behavior. The basic idea is that we mirror each other. When someone is harsh to me, I am harsh to them. When someone is critical of me, I am critical of them. When someone judges me, I judge them. It creates a cycle where violence begets more violence and pain begets more pain.

In the Sermon on the Mount, Jesus calls us to something different. He calls us to break the cycle. *Do not judge, so that you will not be judged.* Breaking the cycle means that we have to respond with noncomplementary behavior. In complementary behavior, you give what you get, but in noncomplementary behavior, you give the opposite of what you get. You get bad—criticism, judgment, unfairness. But you give good—compassion, empathy, kindness. I am not advocating letting others trample you, but I am advocating flipping the script, taking them off guard, and disrupting the machine.

The antidote to judgment seems to be compassion—for ourselves and others. Compassion leads to curiosity, to understanding, and to kindness. Compassion is not weakness. Instead, compassion channels the strength, power, wisdom, and grace of God to recognize that even our harshest critics are people made in the image of God. Compassion makes love, even for our enemy, possible.

Prayer: God, you are a chain-breaker, a cycle-disruptor, a change-agent. Equip me for that same work, so that even when I am under fire, I stand strong and firm. Arm me with indiscriminate love that seeks no conditions, that knows no bounds, and that crosses enemy lines; in the name of Jesus. Amen.

Brandi Tevebaugh Horton

Let us say that to offer the hardest blessing, we will need the deepest grace; that to forgive the sharpest pain, we will need the fiercest love; that to release the ancient ache, we will need new strength for every day.[3]

—*Jan Richardson*

A few years back, I experienced the deepest pain of my professional life. It left me feeling powerless and incredibly hurt. I was asked to simply walk away. In it, I lost relationships with colleagues, church members, and an important mentor.

Needless to say, I've had to work a lot on dealing with those hurts. I pray about the hurt, resentment, and loss of what was. I've mourned the loss of relationships I treasured. In my praying and my working, I have found some peace and healing. Enough that I sometimes think I'm past it.

Then I go to an event where I inevitably run across some of the people who were involved. Or, more accurately, I avoid them to the best of my ability. In my avoidance, I know the truth—I'm not fully healed. I haven't forgiven completely. I have more work to do.

I've learned I can't do the work of forgiveness on my own. I need a deeper grace and a fiercer love than what I can muster, so I turn back to God and back to prayer. While I sometimes can't even fathom redemption for my wounds, through prayer and song I am reminded of God's incredible, abiding love; and through relationships, I have friends who will attentively listen and share hugs and tears. In all this, God administers a healing balm that is greater than the sharpest pain.

Finding forgiveness for those days isn't to condone what happened. It isn't to justify injustice. It is asking God to enable me to move past the anger, hurt, and resentment so I might move freely into whatever future God has planned. And hopefully, one day, I can stand in the presence of old pain without feeling compelled to move away.

Prayer: God of healing, renewal, and redemption, give me the power to forgive, the power to heal from the past. I know I don't have to be reconciled, I don't have to return to hurtful people, but I need to let go of the pain so I can move freely in this world. Grant me courage and wisdom. Bless me with joy and hope to look beyond my scars; through Jesus Christ the great Redeemer. Amen.

Debbie Sperry

People in Zion, who live in Jerusalem, you will weep no longer.
God will certainly be merciful to you. Hearing the sound of your
outcry, God will answer you. Though the Lord gives you the
bread of distress and the water of oppression, your teacher will
no longer hide, but you will see your teacher. If you stray to the
right or the left, you will hear a word that comes from behind
you: "This is the way; walk in it."

—*Isaiah 30:19-21*

There she is again. That voice—sometimes a whisper, often a shout—leading me down the path of betrayal.

You're not good enough. You're not strong enough. You're not smart enough. Can you really do this job? It's probably easier if you just go ahead and give up now.

Loving God, I know you and I know your truth. Help me shush this critic that resides within, even though I do not welcome her. Remind me of the grace, leadership, and strength countless women before me have displayed through your mercy. Even though I taste the bread of distress and the water of oppression, I believe that you have prepared a new feast for me.

When this voice tells me that my fight for justice won't make a difference, may the God of Compassion remind me that each of my actions have meaning, even if by my actions alone injustice can't be overcome. "This is the way; walk in it."

When she brings about disbelief in my ability to lead, may the God of Mercy remind me that I am called because of who I am and whose I am. May I rest in the confidence that I am capable.

When she challenges my strength and beauty, falsely believing that I should be more like others and less like myself, may the God of Love remind me that I am created in your image, and that at my creation you called me very good. May the mercy of God always speak loudest in my heart.

Prayer: Dear God, I pray to believe now that the voices of criticism are not authentic to who I am. When my inner critic seeks to speak more loudly than the truth I know rests in my heart, may I remember that you have claimed me and called me beloved. Give me the strength to shush that voice, so that my mind and heart may be filled with your grace. And even if the voice still lingers, remind me that all of who I am, inner critic and all, is someone you welcome as a coworker for your kin-dom, being made real here on earth as it is in heaven. Amen.

Mara LeHew Bailey

⌒ A Prayer for Letting Go ⌒ of White Fragility

God, I never intended this. This is not where I thought this would go. And now I have this pit in my stomach. I've been found out. I'm called out.

Jesus, it's not my fault. It can't be. Can it? Well, maybe, a little. Just a little my fault. But not my intention! Can't they see that I'm a good person?

Spirit of Truth, tell them what a good person I am. I'm not like those other people, those bad people, the ones I protest against. I'm not racist. Am I?

O great I AM, you know me. You really know me. You know my faults. You know my sin. And I did this. I messed up. I did.

Christ, I'm stuck in my whiteness. I need to be called out. I don't do the good I want to do. I do the very things that I hate. Forgive me, for I did not know. Now I know. Now I can change.

Thank you, Discerning Spirit. Thank you for the people who call me out. Thank you for the chance to do better. Thank you for teaching me. Thank you for humbling me.

God, keep waking me up. Jesus, show me how to make amends. Holy Spirit, give me courage to repent. Amen.[4]

Diane M. Kenaston

As he came near and saw the city, he wept over it, saying, "If you, even you, had only recognized on this day the things that make for peace! But now they are hidden from your eyes."

—*Luke 19:41-42 NRSV*

G rief. Anger. Sorrow. Loneliness. Joy. Frustration.

I have cried in response to each of these emotions. I have always had a complicated relationship with my tears. Like many women, I have been told to not cry at work, in front of my child, in leadership meetings, and to stuff down the tears that betray all the things my heart wants to shout.

When we are most honest with ourselves, we may struggle to reconcile a Savior who is fully divine and fully human. In seasons of my life I am drawn to the fully divine Jesus who has the tearful reaction that many of us know: "Jesus began to weep" (John 11:35 NRSV). It is logical and comforting to us that Jesus, Offspring of God, weeps at the death of his friend. Grief is hard and holy.

As Jesus weeps over Jerusalem, we take a harder look at this Savior of ours. As humans, we shed tears in response to feelings, and we cry from our ducts and our guts and our lower backs when our emotions overcome us. What is it about Jerusalem, though, that causes Jesus to not just cry but weep?

Jesus looks at the place which held such promise to him. Those he loved had traveled with him, and as he looked over the city he saw all that had befallen it. Was he sad? Was he angry? Did he feel helpless? We may never know. What we do know is that his visceral human response was to weep.

Our tears can be our prayers, if we let them. Our tears occupy the holy space when words fail us. In joy, in sorrow, in the face of injustice, and in the mixture of emotions that is impossible to be named, we weep body-shaking tears like Jesus did.

When peace was absent from his sight, Jesus wept. May we unashamedly shed the tears that well up within us when peace is absent from our spirits, from our communities, and from our world.

Prayer: God who shed salty tears at the death of peace, let my own tears fall upon the fertile soil of your creation. May the warmth of your Spirit nurture all the possibilities that lay dormant so that your peace will grow all around me. Amen.

Anna Guillozet

But Jael, Heber's wife, picked up a tent stake and a hammer.
While Sisera was sound asleep from exhaustion, she tiptoed to
him. She drove the stake through his head and down into the
ground, and he died. Just then, Barak arrived after chasing
Sisera. Jael went out to meet him and said, "Come and I'll show
you the man you're after." So he went in with her, and there was
Sisera, lying dead, with the stake through his head.

—Judges 4:21-22

She would have nothing to do with me. In my new job, I had replaced an adult who walked with her through the worst time in her life. No matter what I did, I wasn't the person she wanted to talk to. It made for a difficult start to a new job—coming in with people mad at me because of who I wasn't. In those moments, I held fast to who I am—without bowing to who I wasn't. I shared my passion, my excitement, and my authentic self.

One day, being authentic meant sharing one of my favorite Bible stories—a story that is rarely preached and that she certainly didn't know. Judges 4 tells the story of Deborah, a woman raised to be a military leader and one who brings God's justice. Deborah's not alone, however. Jael, another woman in the fight, is the one to dispatch Sisera, the oppressive ruler overpowering the Israelites. Jael invites him into her tent—using her femininity to gain access to him—before striking a tent peg to his head, killing him.

As predicted, she had never heard of Jael. As I shared the story, the walls came down between us. This ancient story—shared authentically and hopefully—became the catalyst for something new to be born between us. I am not her, and I never will be, but that is ok, because I am me—fully and authentically me. This is the power of showing up as our whole and authentic selves.

Criticism need not hold us back from being totally who we are. Even when that criticism might be valid, even when it might help us be "better," we can be transformed by entering into relationships as our full and authentic selves, while inviting other people to do the same.

Prayer: Knowing God, you know my heart and the hearts of those who criticize me. May I be strengthened in who I am and formed into the woman you call me to be. Amen.

J. Paige Boyer

Living Gratitude

Being grateful isn't easy. In a world where bad news travels at the speed of tweets and the twenty-four-hour news cycle, there's always a lot to be the opposite of grateful for. All around us we see work to do: systems that need tearing down, people that need building up, and institutions that suck the life out of us. Finding something to be grateful for is a challenge. Living gratitude is an act of defiance.

These days it seems like everyone is talking about the benefits of gratitude. We often hear that we should make a list of five things every day for which we are grateful. We hear that this helps to train us to look for things that make us grateful and shifts our perspective. According to the Yale Center for Emotional Intelligence, "Unlike other positive emotions like hope and happiness, gratitude is inherently relational: it reaches past the person experiencing it and into the social realm. It is gratitude in large measure that inspires people to acts of kindness, since it's natural to respond to gifts with heartfelt gifts of your own. And that strengthens your bonds with other people."[1] It is clear that many people find the practice of finding things for which to be grateful a life-changing practice.

Keeping a list, while good practice, is different than living gratitude, however. To live gratitude is to set the terms for our own lives rather than to be passive consumers of how others would have us live. To live gratitude is to see first where God is, in a world where people are always in our faces.

Living gratitude is embodying gratitude, not picking a few things every day for which we are grateful, but rather setting gratitude as the way we show up in our lives. Christians know this is possible because our entire cosmos exists because it is a gift from a Creator God. Imprinted with the image of God, as the Bible says in Genesis 1:26, we can live with gratitude as our frame of reference for everything else.[2]

In the pages of this section, you will find the very real struggles of women. You will not read the words of women who are trying to pretend like nothing is wrong or who think gratitude is putting on a happy face. You will read the words of women who, despite everything, can't help but see God's presence and blessing everywhere.

Make no mistake, this is difficult. We have to fight to see the world around us as God's. We have to fight to see ourselves as God's beloved children. We often have to fight against prejudices that would have us see others as less than God's beloved children. In order to defy seeing the world as nothing but hopeless, we must enter the fray with God by our side and commit to living gratefully.

Emily A. Peck-McClain

When Eve bit into the apple, she gave us the world as we know
the world—beautiful, flawed, dangerous, full of being. . . .
Without Eve there would be no utopias, no imaginable reason to
find and to create transcendence, to ascend toward the light. Eve's
legacy to us is the imperative to desire. Babies and poems are born
in travail of this desire, her great gift to the loveable world.[3]

—*Barbara Grizzuti Harrison*

Raise a glass of apple juice to the first audacious bitch. I am grateful for Eve, and for all who risk everything to find a new way, for those who keep asking questions that bring us closer to God's ideal world.

My humanity is rooted in the ways our flaws breathe air into the most suffocating moments. My humanity is caught up in the ways we wound, heal, forgive, break each other, and find grace again, all while seeking perfect love. I cannot imagine a world devoid of that. For each of my moments of struggle and pain, there has been an opportunity to love beyond measure. I'm grateful I've always found those opportunities.

I don't believe that our pain is worth some magical good on the other side. I believe that sometimes we are given more than we can handle. I believe we often go through more than we can handle alone. I also believe community is rooted more deeply and loves more fiercely when our imperfections seek each other, when we reach out to each other in the lost moments and help find the path forward. Without all of the ways I fall short, what would I reach for?

We speak of Eve's sin as if it removed us from God. But God didn't just choose to create humanity; God chose to become humanity. And so I revel in the midst of imperfect humanity just as Christ did. I want to understand its beauty, just as our Creator does. This creates a fierce love that calls me to stand alongside those who have been harmed by the evil choices of flawed and beloved people. This creates a grace-filled love that helps people see the good that God imbued within them. This creates the desire for more that pushes me to dream, create, fail, and try again. These are experiences of a community called together. These are the experiences of God-as-human. These are the experiences of Eve. I am grateful that Eve's curiosity allowed me to step into a broken world and experience love in its fullest form.

Prayer: Creator God, I am overwhelmed by all that I cannot fix. I give thanks for the passion that calls me to try. Loving Christ, I am heartbroken by all the ways we turn away from your face. I give thanks for the compassion that calls me back. Wild Spirit, I am weary of all of the ways I feel like I've failed too much. I give thanks for all the times you remind me that I am always enough. God of three-in-one, call me together with all audacious seekers of truth; in Christ's name I pray. Amen.

Janessa Chastain

Let the word of Christ dwell in you richly; teach and admonish
one another in all wisdom; and with gratitude in your hearts
sing psalms, hymns, and spiritual songs to God.

—*Colossians 3:16 NRSV*

Finding a place of solace to rest in our Creator's arms is not something that I am particularly good at. Music, however, does allow me to go to a "happy place," to escape, where I can come to Jesus reverently singing praises to him. Allowing lyrics to flow over my being, flooding my soul with peace, is how I find solace. This has been a learned coping mechanism, and has certainly proven itself effective, time and time again.

It proved itself effective in healing as a survivor of sexual trauma. It proved itself effective enduring a drill sergeant's endless taunting. It proved itself effective during arduous convoys through the streets and cities of war-torn Iraq. It proved itself effective amidst barrages of sexist slurs and cynicism from my male counterparts, who were assumed to be my battle buddies. It proved itself effective when I was passed over for a promotion even though I had more qualifications and experience than the other candidate, a male. It proves itself effective still, when my heart and mind begin to race under duress of PTSD.

Even though these times described bring memories of pain, shame, and fear, I am able to look back with gratitude in my heart because through music the words of Christ would wash over me, bringing strength and peace. Through the grace of God and music, I have come to find a place of shelter where my entire being can rest in the arms of our Heavenly Creator.

Prayer: O God, who is my Great Comforter, allow me to harvest gratitude regardless of what life brings, as I sing praises to you. Help me find solace in moments where darkness lies; in your holy and gracious name. Amen.

Quaya Rae Ackerman

⌒ **A Prayer of Gratitude** ⌒
After a Difficult Experience

Thank you, God! It's over!

As I pull away and tears run down my face, be with me, O God.

As I live to tell the story, be with me, O God.

As I learn to move on, be with me, O God.

As I struggle through the horrible words said to me, be with me, O God.

As I face the unknown, be with me, O God.

As this chapter comes to a close, thank you, God

That you never left me,

That I might have bruises, but through your strength, I made it.

Heal me, mold me, and support me.

Help me find a place of living waters to refresh me.

May I bathe in your grace, mercy, and love.

Lead me, Good Shepherd, to new pastures.

Thank you, God! It's over!

Amen.

Ashley Fitzpatrick Jenkins

*Sing to the L*ORD *a new song*
  because he has done wonderful things!
His own strong hand and his own holy arm
  have won the victory!

. . . .

Let all the rivers clap their hands;
  *let the mountains rejoice out loud altogether before the L*ORD
  because he is coming to establish justice on the earth!
He will establish justice in the world rightly;
  he will establish justice among all people fairly.

—Psalm 98:1, 8-9

Circumstances do not produce gratitude. How many of us know people who live in very fortunate circumstances, and yet they are unhappy? Even in the best of circumstances, they spend their lives grumbling and complaining that the good is not great. At the same time, we all know people who experience challenge after challenge, and they somehow find a way to be grateful in spite of all that is happening around them. It's mind-boggling.

It's nearly impossible to explain either the presence of gratitude or the absence of it just by looking at someone's circumstances. Gratitude has far more to do with what's happening on the inside than it does with what's happening on the outside.

One of the most powerful examples that we have of this is found through reading the psalms. The Book of Psalms was compiled when the Israelites were living in exile under the thumb of the Babylonians. Life was hard for them.

And yet, even in the midst of such difficult circumstances, the psalmist chose gratitude. The psalmist chose to celebrate both the things that God had done in the past and the things that God would do in the future.

Giving thanks wasn't just a response. Giving thanks was a choice, an orientation toward life, and a posture developed over time. How do we become more thankful people who function out of a posture of gratitude? I think it starts with practice.

Today, I encourage you to practice. Perhaps, begin by asking yourself these questions:

- What wonderful things has God done in my life in the past? Pause and give thanks.
- What challenges am I facing today? Pause and give thanks.
- What wonderful things will God do in the future? Pause and give thanks.

Like the psalmist, take time today to pause and give thanks regardless of your circumstances.

Prayer: Loving God, thank you for all of the wonderful things that you have done in my life. Thank you for your never-ending presence with me as I face challenges today. Thank you for all of the wonderful things that you will do in the future. Help me develop a posture of gratitude no matter my circumstances. Amen.

Sara M. Nelson

From now on, brothers and sisters, if anything is excellent and
if anything is admirable, focus your thoughts on these things: all
that is true, all that is holy, all that is just, all that is pure, all
that is lovely, and all that is worthy of praise.

—Philippians 4:8

I can be a worrier. Sometimes without realizing it, I find myself fearing people think the worst about me. I find myself fearing that the future is bleak. I find myself thinking pessimistically but believing I'm just being realistic, as if reality is the way I see it. Becoming aware of these patterns has been a big part of my journey over the years.

Lately I have been reading about how our brains are constantly being rewired. This means we can direct our thoughts and behaviors to physically impact what neurons fire in our brains. These developments in neuroscience are leading psychologists to help people live better lives.

A look at the Bible suggests that this concept is not new. Paul urges early Christians, who were living through moments of conflict and unease, to focus on what is pure, true, and praiseworthy. Just prior to this encouragement, Paul urges them to rejoice, knowing that God is near (Philippians 4:4-5). Paul urges them to give their worries to God in trust (Philippians 4:6-7).

In the midst of challenging situations, these verses from Philippians have become a spiritual lifeline. They help catch me when my brain spirals into worrying, second-guessing, or doubting myself and other people. They help me redirect my thoughts toward God and toward the good, not as a way of denying problems, but as a way of remembering that God is present in every moment, waiting for me to see, trust, and ground myself in that God-steeped reality. From lived awareness of God's trustworthiness and of the good news that God is always near, I can face what comes with a hope that counters despair and a gratitude that counters fear.

Prayer: Ever-present God, make me aware of habits that cloud my ability to serve you with gratitude for your presence and hope for your possibilities. Ground me in your steady love, truth, and grace. Guide me to focus on what is excellent, admirable, true, holy, just, pure, lovely, and worthy of praise. Amen.

Alison VanBuskirk Philip

A Prayer of Gratitude for Wisdom

Lord, I confess that sometimes it is hard to live with gratitude: When the days are long. When people are complaining. When things don't go as planned. When life seems too chaotic, too consumed with stress. When I just want to curl up in bed and try again tomorrow, come Lord Jesus.

Come and renew. Come and revive. Come and reveal yourself again to remind me that your mercies are new every morning. Come and sweep over my heart with a spirit of gratitude for that which I have overlooked or missed.

Let that gratitude take root and bear fruit: Love, for the people and community I count as mine. Joy, even when things are not going as I hope. Peace, in times of chaos. Gentleness, with myself and others. Faithfulness, to keep on keeping on.

May all that you have blessed me with, especially on the hard days, break through the cracks in my life and shine forth your glory.

Amen.[4]

Michelle Bodle

*It is good to give thanks to the L*ORD,
   to sing praises to your name, Most High;
   to proclaim your loyal love in the morning,
      your faithfulness at nighttime.

                                              —*Psalm 92:1-2*

I find it easy to give thanks in the morning, when the day is just dawning and everything feels new and full of possibility. Then, life happens: the kids start whining, injustice saturates the news, organizational dynamics at work rear their ugly heads, and demands on my time start piling up, pulling me in several directions at once. When my mind is uncluttered, it's easy to give thanks for what has been and for what is to come, confident in God's love and faithfulness. But as I move into the day, struggles and stress weigh me down, and gratitude becomes more challenging.

However, the month my daughter turned three, she taught me to give thanks in the evening too. Our church engaged in a daily gratitude practice for the month of November, recording the things each family member was thankful for at the end of every day. On November 1, I approached this practice wondering if my young child would be able to understand and participate. What I didn't realize was that she would be able to contribute fully while I often struggled to practice gratitude at the end of the day. I found myself overcomplicating the practice by trying to name something deeply meaningful each night; my daughter's gratitude was simple and to the point. She was thankful for playing outside, a cookie, and time to snuggle. I realized that even after all the hard stuff of the day has piled up, I can be grateful for simple things too: lovely weather, a hot cup of coffee, or a meeting that ended early. I discovered that my gratitude for simple things helped me refocus on God and others.

One day that November, I thanked my husband for cooking dinner. This is a task we share, but on that particular day, I was grateful that he had done it. Then, our daughter thanked him for cooking dinner. Now, we have a practice of thanking whoever cooked dinner that night. It's a simple expression of gratitude that makes a huge difference. Practicing gratitude at the end of the day taught me to say thank you to God and others more often, for big things and small things, and to recognize God's faithfulness in the midst of the mundane, even at the end of the day.

Prayer: Gracious God, thank you for your love and faithfulness in all things, big and small. Open my eyes to your work in the world around me: morning, evening, and all day long. Help me live with a grateful heart each and every day. Amen.

Jessica Petersen

I always put the LORD in front of me;
*   I will not stumble because he is on my right side.*
That's why my heart celebrates and my mood is joyous;
*   yes, my whole body will rest in safety*
*   because you won't abandon my life to the grave;*
*   you won't let your faithful follower see the pit.*

You teach me the way of life.
*   In your presence is total celebration.*
Beautiful things are always in your right hand.

—Psalm 16:8-11

I had my first panic attack when I was seventeen. While attending a concert, the venue's low ceilings and walls suddenly seemed to tighten. This amplified the flashing lights, thumping base, and the throngs of sweaty bodies around me until I felt as though I would be crushed by it all. I bolted for the door, desperate to escape. It was terrifying. And it wasn't my last. Mental exhaustion, threatening encounters, the news I had lost my grandfather . . . it is the same thing every time: My vision narrows. My breath draws shallow. The noises around me grow louder, yet muffled and distant. Panic and fear drive desperate thoughts: Will I ever feel calm again? Will I ever feel safe?

Yes. Eventually. (Thank you, Jesus.)

Ocean water. Mountain air. Worship music (at a volume I can control). A heavy winter blanket. My child's tiny arms. As these things surround and embrace me, my heart rate slows, my eyes trust and close, my breath steadies, and eventually I come back to myself. (I see you, Holy Spirit.)

The writer of the sixteenth psalm understands. She invokes God to surround her, before and beside.[5] With God before her and God beside, she feels rooted, undisturbed by the chaos climaxing all over the room. With God before her and God beside, she is no longer alone. With God before her and God beside, she becomes a triple threat: a woman with a gladdened heart, a rejoicing soul, and (Lord, may it be so) a body at rest. Watch out! That glad heart can now open to the broken ones around her. That rejoicing soul can resist the evil powers at work against her. And that rested body—that beautifully imperfect vessel of incarnational love and mercy—has remembered that it is strong. And in strength she found dignity, and in dignity (Lord, bless her), she remembered her power.

So rest up, Beloved. And don't apologize. Surround yourself with what you need so that you can come back too.

Prayer:
God, go before me. God, stay beside me.
I'm yours.
Lighten my heavy heart.
My soul wants to rejoice.
Help me trust you enough to rest.
You are with me in this.
No matter what.
Show me the way forward.
In you, I find true joy. Amen.

Blair Boyd Zant

∼ A Prayer of Gratitude ∼ When All Else Fails

God, I do not know what to do. I have tried everything. I have begged and pleaded. I have wept. I have been angry and frustrated. I have chased after every resource possible. Yet, I am still here, feeling empty. I am still here praying, talking, trying hard to listen. "Thank you, God" is all that I have left. Thank you, God, for perseverance. Thank you, God, for strength. Thank you for all that was, is, and will be. May the gratitude of this moment carry me and inspire me as I hold on to this life that you have blessed me with. I do not know where else to turn. Thank you for being there, for hearing me, and responding to my prayer with your abundant grace. Amen.

Catherine Christman

*Then the one seated on the throne said, "Look! I'm making all
things new." He also said, "Write this down, for these words are
trustworthy and true."*

—*Revelation 21:5*

We like new things. We like new homes that are move-in ready.
New clothes. New shoes. New hair. We like new stores in cute
new neighborhoods, even though it is likely a gentrified old neighborhood
bearing a new name. We even like the way a new car smells; we like it so
much that we buy the new-car scent to make our old cars smell new again.
We like new things, but *all* things new?

The truth is, even though I like new things, I often hold tight to the
old. I catch myself engaging in old behaviors, narratives, and thoughts that
no longer serve me but are just so damn comfortable. It can be comfortable
to play small, to not apply for the promotion, to remain silent in the midst
of conflict and to have the same hairstyle since high school. Yet, what I
also know is that when I hold too tightly to the old and the comfortable,
I am settling and missing opportunities to fully embrace God's infinite
possibilities in my life.

Each day that I take a moment to look back on how far I've come, I am
overwhelmed with gratitude. When I let go of doubt and embrace confidence, when I speak up, when I wear bright red lipstick, when I say yes to
goodness—I thank God for the old and all of the new. It hasn't been easy,
but it has absolutely been worth it. God has been "trustworthy and true"
along every step of this journey. Our faith, our hope is built on a God who
is making all things new!

*Prayer: Dear God, when I find myself holding tightly to the old, please remind
me that you are Alpha and Omega. When I begin to get too comfortable and
settle for less, remind me that I can trust your promises. God of new and infinite
possibilities, thank you. Amen.*

Theresa S. Thames

*He was trying to see who Jesus was, but, being a short man,
he couldn't because of the crowd. So he ran ahead and climbed
up a sycamore tree so he could see Jesus, who was about to pass
that way. When Jesus came to that spot, he looked up and said,
"Zacchaeus, come down at once. I must stay in your home today." So Zacchaeus came down at once, happy to welcome Jesus.
Everyone who saw this grumbled, saying, "He has gone to be the
guest of a sinner."*

—Luke 19:3-7

My mother is an amazing woman. She has been through hell and back time and time again. She always comes out stronger and more determined on the other side. Her personality is one that some might call stubborn. She has been plagued with one health crisis after another. She has a head injury which has left her with a mental disability. She is an addict and compulsive gambler. Yet, she is one of the rock stars in my life.

The world has turned its back on her many times over her lifetime. Her church has viewed her as a problem. Her job and legal history do not make it easy for her to hold down a career. Her health impacts her day-to-day living, not to mention her relationships with our family and my father.

When I ask her about her life, faith, and who Jesus is to her, she immediately talks about gratitude. She speaks of gratitude for the next generation in our family. She speaks of thanksgiving for my father, my brother and me and our spouses, and for her own mother for standing by her when the darkest of days have come. She speaks of her pastor caring for her as if she was family. She speaks of Jesus, who gave her perseverance to survive weeks in jail, strength to stand under the weight of a cancer diagnosis, and peace of mind to know that the church as an institution is not perfect when it turned its back on her for her mistakes.

Mom is also kind of short, like Zacchaeus was. I imagine her experience would be similar to his with Jesus and the crowd. Zacchaeus was a sinner by both the world's definition and his own admission. When the crowd was grumbling as Jesus called for him, I am certain Zacchaeus's heart became full of gratitude. Living gratitude is offering thanksgiving in the middle of every aspect of life. It is not some future plan to offer praise and worship to God, like next Sunday or when things in life get better. It is offering thanks in the moment and in the middle of real life. Zacchaeus is proof that no matter what, God knows the heart. Living gratitude is giving thanks that God sees beyond all that we are to see what we can be.

Prayer: God, thank you for knowing my heart. Thank you for seeing beyond my faults, failures, and mistakes. As I seek to practice living gratitude, remind me of Zacchaeus and all the others that the world has said are not good enough. Remind me of all those you called to your side, and help me picture myself among them. Amen.

Catherine Christman

*The ship of my life may or may not be sailing on calm and ami-
able seas. The challenging days of my existence may or may not
be bright and promising. Stormy or sunny days, glorious or lonely
nights, I maintain an attitude of gratitude. If I insist on being
pessimistic, there is always tomorrow. Today I am blessed.*[6]

—*Maya Angelou*

When we think about gratitude, we often think about what we have in comparison to what others lack. We say things like, "I am grateful for this food because there are those who don't have any," or, "I thank God for my health because I know a couple of friends who just got diagnosed with cancer." We continue to compare ourselves to those around us even when we are giving thanks to God. We have all done it; we do it mindlessly! What does that say about our gratitude? When we catch ourselves saying a prayer of thanksgiving that comes from this place of comparison, it is important to stop and redirect our gratitude.

Living in gratitude is not easy because it involves recognizing that we have enough. In a capitalist country like the United States that claims a kind of civic Christianity, it can be hard to see that God's blessings are not rewarded according to merit. It's in the DNA of the United States to see all events, both good and bad, as part of God's system of reward and punishment—reward to those who are "faithful Christians" and punishment to those who are "sinners." This kind of thinking creeps into our subconscious. It convinces us that we should be thankful that we are not worse off than we are and that tomorrow we should do better. It enslaves us into a system that privileges those who hold power and discriminates against those who sit in the margins.

Redirecting gratitude enables us to be thankful for what we have done with God by our side. In this place, celebrate your triumphs and your failures. Know that God is with you every step of the way, even when you feel alone, because there are times when you do feel alone.

Prayer: Transcending Spirit, Loving Parent, thank you for the many times you have held me in love, even when I have failed you. Thank you for the communities that surround me and confirm your presence by lifting me up when I fear I can no longer keep going. I acknowledge that I am enough and that I have enough. As I look at my life's present, past, and future, I see your wildfire embracing me every step of the way. I see the works of your Spirit guiding me through the wilderness and bringing me back to you when I deviate from your path. Help me continue to work for justice for my siblings who are being persecuted, discriminated, and hurt. I rejoice in thanksgiving, knowing you hear my prayer and delight in me; in the name of the Creator, the Redeemer, and the Sustainer. Amen.

Cassandra Núñez

A Prayer of Gratitude
for the Unexpected

God of surprises and the unexpected, my heart is filled with gratitude for all that has happened. In the midst of the unexpected, I am reminded of your constant presence, guiding and sustaining me in every moment. All I can do is say thank you: for yesterday, for today, and for tomorrow.

Holy God, in the midst of this unexpected surprise, I lift my prayers for peace in the midst of the unknown. I ask for strength to find my voice, to love fiercely, and to live boldly. With gratitude for your presence, I will face the future unafraid to transform the world, diving into the unexpected and following where you lead. Most of all, I lift my prayer of gratitude for the ways that you continue to show up in my life—in the unexpected and in the things I plan. Giving thanks for every unexpected surprise, I pray in the name of Jesus Christ and through the power of your Holy Spirit. Amen.

Lorrin M. Radzik

I was very glad in the Lord because now at last you have shown
concern for me again. (Of course you were always concerned but
had no way to show it.)

—Philippians 4:10

One of my least favorite verses to see emblazoned on a shirt is Philippians 4:13: "I can do all things through Christ who strengthens me" (NKJV). It has always conjured images of Popeye squeezing open his can of spinach and suddenly being muscular and winning the day. Maybe for some people, this verse gives them the ability to endure hardships. But not me. I never found instant strength and confidence in this verse. And I don't think that's what Paul was feeling, either.

I see the appeal of reducing Paul's struggle to a triumphant slogan, but actually reading Philippians reminds me that Paul is writing not from a position of strength but from one of weakness. He is imprisoned and out of options to make things happen for himself.

Yet even then, Paul gives thanks for the community of faith that is showing concern in his moment of need. Far from this passage being a declaration of personal victory, it is a thank-you note to the community that is keeping him alive.

Rather than a shout of victory, this passage is like a sigh of calm resignation. Paul is not triumphant, nor is he hardship-trolling. He is resigned to his weakness and is showing his beloved Philippians what he means by the foolishness of the cross: that despite how bad things are, he is not hopeless nor ashamed. Paul knows any strength he has is not his own, but rather is Christ's. It manifests in the love and care of a community of believers.

In times of struggle and vulnerability, I have relied on a community of women to show up and carry me in my weakness. I don't need slogans or quick fixes to pump me up and assure me I will triumph. I need people who can see that things are hard, and who can offer help. It is through this kind of community that I find the kind of peace I see with Paul.

In my weakness, the collective strength of others sustains me because we share a common hope: Jesus, who gives us his strength. The shared care of the community gives me peace and endurance more than any Bible verse on a shirt ever could.

Prayer: Loving and Constant God, thank you for the women who carry me in my weakness. Thank you for their faith and concern for me. In my weakness, remind me I am not alone or abandoned. Help me accept what is offered without pride. Lead me on the road to peace. Amen.

Laura C. Patterson

*To become fully human means learning to turn my gratitude for
being alive into some concrete common good. It means growing
gentler toward human weakness. It means practicing forgiveness
of my and everyone else's hourly failures to live up to divine
standards.*[7]

—*Barbara Brown Taylor*

Stop saying *I'm sorry.*" This is a constant refrain from one my best friends.
I have been conditioned to apologize for everything, all the time, and
she's trying to get me to stop.

Even when I have worked hard to stop saying those two little—and
belittling—words, I never knew what to say instead. *I'm sorry* became as
instinctual as *um* or *like*. I needed new words.

Artist Yao Xiao was one of the first people I saw who suggested a good
replacement for these words: *Thank you.*[8]

This strategy has helped me to save *I'm sorry* for the times when it is
truly needed, such as when I've harmed someone or when I need to make
confession and begin the work of reconciliation.

This linguistic change has also had another unexpected benefit: I am
able to express gratitude for the ways the people in my life have accepted
me in my wholeness and are gentler to my weaknesses.

Saying "thank you for waiting" instead of "Sorry, I'm late" acknowledges the grace my friends have extended for my lateness. "Thank you for
your patience" names the time people have given me when our rhythms
aren't the same.

Saying *thank you* raises up another instead of putting myself down. Instead of making myself smaller with a misplaced *I'm sorry*, saying *thank you*
reminds me that I am blessed with people in my life who love me, just as
I am.

Prayer: Thank you, God, for those people who have helped me know my worth. Thank you for giving me the courage to live into that value, and thank you for your forgiveness for the times I have made myself smaller instead of living into my whole and beloved self. Amen.

J. Paige Boyer

A Prayer When You're Not Grateful

Listen, God. I hear that I'm supposed to be grateful all the time, even when things are really hard. I'm here praying to you today because I'm not grateful. I have no idea why or for how long things will be so hard. I'm tired and I'm angry and I'm hanging on by a thread . . . so I'm sure not grateful. There might be some blessing in disguise. I might emerge from this stronger than I can imagine one day. I may look back one day and laugh. Today is not that day.

So here's the deal: You hold onto that thread for me. You bring me people to help me through this. You wake me up tomorrow with some kind of strength I don't have today. I need you. I'm counting on you.

And if tomorrow is just as hard, I'm going to be right here praying this prayer again tomorrow night. Let me rest tonight, and I'll be grateful for rest. Help me make it through another twenty-four hours, and I'll be grateful then. I'm not grateful now, but I hope I will be soon.

That's all I've got.

Amen.

Emily A. Peck-McClain

I wanted to have something good to remember about today. . . .
Sometimes you have to provide such moments yourself.[9]

—*Tamora Pierce*

Revolution is hard, painful work. You've heard it just as I have: don't help strangers; they're scamming you. Don't stop and help; they'll hurt you. Don't help a coworker; they'll take advantage of you. Don't help. Don't give. Don't trust. Hoard your money. Keep it all to yourself. "They" might hurt you. Don't trust them; they'll sell you out. Don't expect gratitude; nobody will notice the work you do. Our world and oftentimes our own natures push us to self-interest and fear. There's never enough of that proverbial pie.

But there's a revolution in generosity.

A revolution in caring.

A revolution in giving of ourselves.

A generous life *is* a revolution.

God calls us to a life of giving of ourselves. We help and we give, not because the world deserves it, but because we must put gratitude into the world ourselves. We give because God gave first. Generosity is not only about money but also about giving goodness.

Revolution can be the overthrow of systems of oppression or even the shattering of one more glass ceiling. When we are generous with our kindness and our goodness, this generosity comes back to us in a way that feeds our own souls. We know there is goodness in the world because we stand beside God and create it together. We are grateful for the ability to do good.

When we are generous with our goodness both as revolution and in the midst of revolution, we find ourselves surrounded by opportunities to be grateful. A revolution of generosity is a revolution of goodness. This revolution is not up to us alone, but we may have to begin it. If we don't, who will? When the world keeps throwing crap our way, let us be grateful for our ability to throw good back.

Prayer: God, stand beside me when I'm feeling alone. Help me be grateful even when I see a harsh world. Help me be grateful for my ability to do good alongside you. Amen.

Sara McManus

Then a woman who had been bleeding for twelve years came up behind Jesus and touched the hem of his clothes. She thought, if I only touch his robe I'll be healed. When Jesus turned and saw her, he said, "Be encouraged, daughter. Your faith has healed you." And the woman was healed from that time on.

—*Matthew 9:20-22*

Once, when I was in a season of disciplined practice of silence and stillness, these words came to life for me in a vision that was as real as anything I have ever experienced.

In this vision, I was the woman. After enough years in leadership to reach burnout, but far too few years to exhaust a career or a calling, I was groveling in the dust. I was too weary to care about the crowd stepping on me (again), and I was desperate to touch the hem of Jesus's garment. Nothing else had worked—not rest or doctors or spiritual practices or self-care. I suddenly recognized how desperate I was for my spirit to be healed of the particular emptiness and loneliness (even in a crowd, especially in a crowd) that women in leadership know all too well.

The outcome of my vision differs from the biblical story. When Jesus passed right by my outstretched arm, I didn't feel a thing. I failed to touch the hem of his clothes. When the excitement of the crowd passed me by, I knew he was gone. I left my arm outstretched for as long as I could, still hoping, I suppose, to grab hold of something that would save me. When I didn't have the strength to keep reaching, I lay there in the dust, weeping. I wept until the crowd departed, and I was all alone with only dust, my tears, and the mud resulting from the combination of the two. When I finally looked up, I wasn't alone after all. Jesus had come back to the spot where I had dissolved into tears, the place where I had both sought his help and given up on receiving it.

It was faith that empowered this biblical woman to reach out. It was her story and other women who came before me that taught me to reach out, too, and to trust that I would not be left without that reach being returned.

I am grateful for Jesus who still passes through city streets, and especially for the moments when I recognize him. I am grateful for Jesus, who backtracks to be present with me until I can follow him forward again. I am grateful for women throughout the ages who dare to reach out, speak up, and encourage me with their lives of faith.

Be encouraged, daughter. Even faith that can envision reaching out is enough to bring about healing.

Prayer: Jesus, even when you seem beyond my grasp, I am never out of reach of your healing presence. Thank you for holy visions, for women who model faith, and for the evolving gift of wholeness. Amen.

Karen Hernandez

~ A Prayer to Be Grateful When You ~ Really Just Want to Be Hateful

Confession time, God. Sometimes I just can't even. I don't want to play nice or put up with the unspoken and unjust rules that hinder the oppressed and elevate those in power. My frustration, resentment, and anger quickly gain fury like a maelstrom. When that happens, I can't see. I can't feel. I can't hear. I can't be. I want to be hateful.

It's happening now. I am a hot mess where, in an effort to triage my breaking heart, I am growing desensitized to the goodness and blessing of life around me.

Help me, please.

Renew my senses. Help me connect with my own spirit, the world, and you, so that I can once again be reminded of the wondrous miracle of life itself. Pour your healing and refreshing grace into the churning fire of my frustration. Pour life into these broken, fractured pieces of my soul. Nourish my longing to appreciate all that surrounds me. Resurrect my spirit through the power of gratitude, that through gratitude your Creative Spirit will connect with mine, bringing life and new possibilities.

Amen.

Nicole de Castrique Jones

Mary got up and hurried to a city in the Judean highlands. She entered Zechariah's home and greeted Elizabeth. When Elizabeth heard Mary's greeting, the child leaped in her womb, and Elizabeth was filled with the Holy Spirit. With a loud voice she blurted out, "God has blessed you above all women, and he has blessed the child you carry. Why do I have this honor, that the mother of my Lord should come to me? As soon as I heard your greeting, the baby in my womb jumped for joy. Happy is she who believed that the Lord would fulfill the promises he made to her."

—Luke 1:39-45

L ast year, I received unimaginable bad news. My only two children—one an infant, the other a preschooler—were diagnosed with a fatal neuromuscular disease. For months, I was so consumed by anxiety and depression that I couldn't eat, sleep, or concentrate on simple tasks, nor could I give my full attention to the congregation I shepherd. I was overcome with fear for the future. I imagined it to be one filled with only sorrow and death, as if all the joy had been sucked out of my life, like air from a balloon. What possible joy could I experience now? How could I be grateful to God amid such grief?

Elizabeth endured years of infertility, walking her own sorrowful, isolating journey before receiving the gift of her son, John. Her relative, Mary, was blindsided with both the task and honor of carrying Christ. Both women's hearts would one day be pierced with grief at the loss of their sons. But in this moment, these two women experienced the miraculous movement of the Holy Spirit within them. For just a moment, they felt the joy of God's power breaking in and filling their souls, inspiring Elizabeth to become the first woman in Luke's gospel to proclaim the identity of Jesus as Messiah. Filled with the Holy Spirit, Elizabeth pronounced a blessing upon Mary, grateful for this experience of God's grace.

A few months after my sons' diagnoses, I began to recite these words:

"We're OK today." Although simple, even cliché perhaps, these words re-orient my heart toward the present, which is an overpowering act of grace in my life. For just a moment, the flood of sorrow is held at bay, and I can find solace in my baby's laugh, my preschooler's enthusiastic singing, and my husband's embrace. I can find gratitude in God's care and compassion through a card offering prayer, a hug from a parishioner, or a call from my pediatrician just to see how I am coping. I now understand that if a moment of joy is all that I have, then I will give thanks to God for that moment—however fleeting it might be. I will bask in the movement of the Holy Spirit within me that fuels me for the arduous journey ahead.

Prayer: God of hope, I am grateful for your steadfast presence in my life. Some-times it feels like the death-dealing blows of life will overwhelm me, so I pray you will break through the sorrow with moments of healing joy. Fill me with your powerful Spirit, that I may proclaim your son as Messiah. Through your son, who knew anguish and death, who overcame it all in the name of your unfathomable love. Amen.

Amelia Beasley

I'm introducing our sister Phoebe to you, who is a servant of the
church in Cenchreae. Welcome her in the Lord in a way that is
worthy of God's people, and give her whatever she needs from
you, because she herself has been a sponsor of many people, myself
included.

—Romans 16:1-2

Sometimes I am asked what is different about my life or job because I am a woman. I realized recently that my answer to that question is often about the difficulties. I have a list: My body is scrutinized all the time. I endure microaggressions constantly. I have been sexually harassed at different workplaces. I have had to fight for maternity leave. I have had to work while feeling nauseated all day long for months on end due to pregnancy. I have had to work harder and prove myself in ways men will never have to. Etc. Etc. I am a cisgender, straight, white woman, so my experience as a woman is not the same as every other woman's, but I bet you have a similar list. Maybe a longer one.

I don't want the struggle to define what it means to be a woman for me. It can't, because there is so much more to being a woman for me. I love being a woman.

This Scripture passage reminds me that from the very beginning, women have been essential to the mission of the church. I have never been the first woman. At none of my jobs—from ice cream scooper to server to minister to professor—have I had to be the first. Even when I have been the first at a job to be a mom of young kids, even when I have been the first to be so young myself, I have never had to be the first.

Paul writes that the Christians in Rome should welcome Phoebe in a way that shows they are God's people because she supports many people, including Paul himself. Oh, that people (and men especially) everywhere would take this to heart! When they welcome women, they should do so in a way that shows they are God's people. Paul entrusted his letter to

Phoebe's care—we have the letter to the Romans in our Bibles because of Phoebe.

Being a woman means I have millions of women ancestors who have gone before me. I am part of a sisterhood that stretches a long way back. Of course I have never been the first.

Prayer: God of all my sisters, the ones all the way back and the ones that will come after me, I thank you for the gifts of women and the gift of my being a woman. Fill my heart with gratitude that I am not alone, but one of many faithful, boundary-breaking women to serve you and your gospel; in the name of your son, a child of a woman, I pray. Amen.

Emily A. Peck-McClain

A Prayer of Gratitude
When You Can't Sleep

Well, here we are again, God. I know I've heard somewhere you neither slumber nor sleep so you know how this feels.[10] Thanks for that. Thanks for everything.

Truly.

I was coming to you with all the crap from this day, but honestly I am just grateful it's over. When I think about how much worse off I'd be without you, I know I'll survive this too. Help me trust that again tomorrow. Help me trust you're with me even when I can't sense you. Help me trust that you forgive me for everything that came from me today when I wasn't following the guidance of your love. Help me trust that even though you're up late with me now, you're also already at work on tomorrow, making sure I'll have everything I need. And most of all, Creator, help me trust that you'll keep taking whatever I have and turn it into something a little bit better. You've done it so many times, so help me remember in the moment that your whole m.o. is taking the awful things of life and squeezing even the tiniest bit of good out of them. So for everything that's swirling through my mind tonight, thank you. Help me see the blessings that will come from even this. And now if it's not too much trouble to ask for one more thing . . . please, Almighty God, help me sleep. Amen.

Corey Tarreto Turnpenny

> *There's a season for everything and a time for every matter under*
> *the heavens: a time for giving birth and a time for dying, a*
> *time for planting and a time for uprooting what was planted, a*
> *time for killing and a time for healing, a time for tearing down*
> *and a time for building up, a time for crying and a time for*
> *laughing, a time for mourning and a time for dancing, a time*
> *for throwing stones and a time for gathering stones, a time for*
> *embracing and a time for avoiding embraces, a time for searching*
> *and a time for losing, a time for keeping and a time for throwing*
> *away, a time for tearing and a time for repairing, a time for*
> *keeping silent and a time for speaking, a time for loving and a*
> *time for hating, a time for war and a time for peace.*
>
> *—Ecclesiastes 3:1-8*

My husband and I struggled with a season of infertility. In the midst of that season, I felt a deep pain that God was taunting me. After all, God placed in me a strong desire to be a mom. Yet no matter what we tried, a negative pregnancy test kept turning up. Doctor's visit after doctor's visit kept us in a cruel cycle of hope and devastating disappointment. Hearing a doctor say "you should be pregnant by now" made the blow of each negative pregnancy test harder to take. It also made my walk with God harder to embrace: How could God do this? Didn't God hear our prayers? Why would God place a desire on my heart that was unattainable?

In the midst of that season, we pursued all avenues available to us to become parents, only to come up short. We moved on to yet another fertility specialist, knowing that if that option failed, we had met the threshold of "failing at all other options" and could let the local adoption agency know that we could officially be added to the waiting-to-adopt list. We were shocked that we didn't end up having to let them know this. After four years, we had a successful fertility treatment, and our daughter joined our family in the fall of 2019.

Now that I am in a new season, I remember that the season of infertility as one I never dreamed we would leave. It felt like it would last forever. Some days, I still wake up forgetting we are in a new season. I find myself between praising God for this child and pondering how this season of infertility is going to continue to shape me and my faith. I find myself praying for other women who continue to struggle in a season of infertility, one that may not end in the kind of season ours did. What will their next season bring that they can't imagine right now? How will God help them become aware of God's presence?

No matter what season of life I am in, I frequently turn to Ecclesiastes 3 for comfort. I continue to turn to these words and hope to live into a better understanding of there being "a season for everything and a time for every matter under the heavens."

Prayer: God of all seasons, give me grace for all seasons in which I find myself. Grant me courage to face whatever season comes next. Cultivate thankfulness in me for all of the seasons I will encounter on my journey by keeping me in the knowledge that there is a season and a time for everything under heaven. Amen.

Lauren A. Godwin

I will give you a new heart and put a new spirit in you. I will remove your stony heart from your body and replace it with a living one.

—Ezekiel 36:26

I know what this feeling is. I have felt it before. The feeling of darkness consuming my being. The hopelessness. The physical heaviness. I know its name: Depression.

You would think that in the midst of depression there would be nothing to be grateful about. But this I know about depression: it is not who I am, but a disease I have. For the generations before me, it was the mark of failure. When my grandmother and great-grandmother suffered from it, doctors could do nothing but send them home, with no way to understand what was wrong. But I know. I know that this too shall pass. I know that there is medication and psychologists who can help it pass. I know that I have depression, but I no longer struggle to accept it.

On bad days, it is easy to rage at God for my living heart that cries too easily at others' pain, that takes on weight for others' problems, that can fall into despair so easily. How often I think it would be easier if my heart were a stone fortress! But my heart that so easily falls to despair is also quick to celebrate joy and love. My living heart can change lives with its compassion.

On days when darkness is invading, I choose not to get swallowed up in despair. I choose to lean into the relationships that soften my heart when it wants to be calloused. I choose to thank God for the people who have worked to treat this monster like the disease that it is. I choose to receive their help. I thank God that I am able to keep going. I thank God that this too shall pass, and that I have the tools to hurry it along. I thank God that I can talk about my depression and encourage others who are still struggling because they don't know its name. Most of all, I thank God that on my worst days, God is still with me, softening my heart.

Prayer: For when it betrays me with sorrow and pain, God, thank you for a living heart. For when it restores me with love and compassion, God, thank you for a living heart. Soften my heart now, that I may feel your presence, and experience your mercy. Amen.

Crystal Jacobson

A Prayer of Gratitude When Living with a Chronic Illness

God, some days it is hard to see the light. I get scared that if this is what it feels like at thirty-two, how will it feel at fifty-two, seventy-two, ninety-two? Will I live to see those years?

Some days I get frustrated when my body or my mind doesn't perform the way I want it to. I expect it to be perfect all the time, but I know that is an unrealistic expectation.

Some days the pain, exhaustion, and other symptoms make it near impossible to get through the day—the unrelenting schedule and ever-present to-do list.

Some days I cry out, "WHY!?"

Some days . . .

But other days:

I live in gratitude that air moves in and out of my lungs.

I live in gratitude that my heart beats.

I live in gratitude that I can work and take care of my family in spite of these illnesses.

I am stronger because of them (not weaker).

And I thank you.

I thank you for healing.

I thank you for the days when the symptoms are less.

I lean on you the days it's overwhelming and frustrating,

and sometimes too painful to bear.

You, God, are my life-giver, my healer, and my comforter. I thank you for all my days.

Amen.

Julia Singleton

But Moses said to the LORD, *"My Lord, I've never been able to speak well, not yesterday, not the day before, and certainly not now since you've been talking to your servant. I have a slow mouth and a thick tongue." Then the* LORD *said to him, "Who gives people the ability to speak? Who's responsible for making them unable to speak or hard of hearing, sighted or blind? Isn't it I, the* LORD? *Now go! I'll help you speak, and I'll teach you what you should say." But Moses said, "Please, my Lord, just send someone else."*

—*Exodus 4:10-13*

Please, my Lord, just send someone else." If I had a dollar for every time I've thought or prayed some form of those words, I'd be rich. And if God had honored my request, my life would look a lot different. Looking back on those times, I'm always grateful that God's plans weren't anything like my own.

When I finished graduate school, my first job was an impossible task. Like many women before me, I was sent into an extremely difficult situation where racism and sexism were alive and well, and I was being asked to clean up someone else's mess. I began the job with the hope and optimism that most of us have when we experience new beginnings, but I quickly learned just how impossible the task was going to be and became discouraged. "Please, my Lord, just send someone else."

That was one of the most difficult years I've experienced, and it was also one of the most important. If I had never been sent to such a difficult place, I never would have uncovered some of the gifts God has given me. In spite of my pleas and prayers to send someone else, God used that experience to help me learn and grow. God used the hardship to develop my passion and skills so that I could serve others in the future. Looking back, all I can do is give thanks to God, knowing I wouldn't be where or who I am today without it.

When we find ourselves echoing the words of Moses, God is there in our midst helping us uncover the gifts we have inside. Once uncovered, watch out world! Who knows what God will do with us and our gifts, if only we let God use us? Thanks be to God that sometimes our desperate, Moses-like pleas are not answered. Imagine what the world would lack without our gifts.

Today, I invite you to give thanks to God for the hard, messy, difficult parts of life. Even in those moments, God is at work in you, uncovering your passion, gifts, and skills so that you can help transform the world.

Prayer: Holy God, thank you for showing up when all I can do is ask you to send someone else. I give you thanks for sending me even when I don't want to go, for trusting me with the work you have called me to do, and for the gifts that I will uncover as I do it. Go with me into the difficult moments, so that I can sense your constant presence. Teach me to live in gratitude for all that I am learning. Amen.

Lorrin M. Radzik

Give thanks in every situation because this is God's will for you
in Christ Jesus.

—1 Thessalonians 5:18

Some mornings I wake up with a smile on my face and a song in my heart. I dance my way into the day, and I'm sure it's going to be a great day—no matter what may come. These days, it is easy to feel grateful.

Other days, well . . . some days it just isn't that easy. Life can be hard, exhausting, and bring grief alongside challenges of depression and anxiety; stress and worry; heartache, uncertainty, and pain.

Life can be really, really hard. On the days we are feeling all of these things, it can be tough to also *feel* grateful. On those days, I admit: verses like this one from 1 Thessalonians frustrate me, because I *know* I should be grateful . . . but that doesn't mean I *feel* it.

Yet the truth is, there is sometimes a chasm between *feeling* grateful and *being* grateful. Even when I don't *feel* it, I can *be* grateful.

One way I practice gratitude is by ending every day with a prayer of thanks. Sometimes, that prayer is long, detailed, and insightful. On hard days, it may just name the breath I take and the clothes I wear. The list doesn't have to be long for me to honor this instruction to give thanks.

The most life-giving practice of gratitude hasn't come from listing off the obvious things, though; it has come in the wrestling. It comes from moments I dive in, in an effort to fake it till I make it. After all, these words don't tell us to give thanks only for that which is good—they tell us to give thanks "in *every* situation."

That means that when I'm mad at my family or had an argument with a friend (again), I recall something about them I love. When facing medical diagnoses that left me numb and fearful, I gave thanks for medical professionals trying to help me . . . and for the people I love who stood beside me in the midst of the unknown.

Whatever may come, whatever we may feel, whatever kind of day we may be having, may we remember the greatest truth of all: God is with us. Sometimes, we don't feel this, either . . . and in those moments, may we be grateful that the light, love, and grace of God are not dependent on how we are *feeling*.

Prayer: Gracious God, on my worst days and on my best, thank you for walking alongside me. Let your presence be known on my darkest of days, and guide me back to you as I seek to give thanks in all that comes my way. Amen.

Jen Tyler

The LORD is my shepherd.
   I lack nothing.
He lets me rest in grassy meadows;
   he leads me to restful waters;
      he keeps me alive.
                  —Psalm 23:1-3a

Every day when I wake up, one of my first practices is to reach for my cell phone. I know, I should probably pray first or engage in some other sort of spiritual discipline . . . but I don't. (Hey! No judgment allowed here!) I reach for my phone. I'm not calling or texting anyone. Instead, I rush to Facebook to see what I missed during the night. Rarely is there a morning when I don't find at least one story that reminds me of the hatred, bigotry, and injustice present in our world. As I encounter those stories, I often want to bury my head beneath the covers and hide from what seems to have become the new normal in our world: hatred rather than love, judgment rather than compassion, war rather than peace. Yet, it is in those same moments that my soul bears witness to the work to which I and so many others like me are called. So I get up and look for the needed strength to face the day.

Psalm 23 is a familiar passage for me. When I was a child, I was confused by the King James Version, which essentially said to my young mind, "The Lord is my shepherd and I don't want him!" In recent years, however, I have come to understand and appreciate the fuller meaning of this text. Now, each morning, as I scroll Facebook my strength is renewed as I reflect on the first three verses of this psalm.

When I am challenged by knowing that my faithfulness to God's call could affect my ability to provide for my basic needs and those of my family, I am comforted in knowing that, because the Lord is my shepherd, my obedience and faithfulness to God will never cause God to be unfaithful to me. When, at the beginning of my day, my spirit has already been made tired by the mayhem wreaking havoc in our communities, I find peace in knowing that my shepherd will allow me to rest in comfortable and nurturing places, just as I fear I am nearing "the edge." When I am fighting for justice amid very real dangers—both revealed and hidden—ever aware that my very life hangs in the balance, I am strengthened by knowing that my shepherd will keep me alive: mind, body, and spirit. I guess it's safe to say that I'm now able to look at Psalm 23 and think to myself with joy, "The Lord is my shepherd and I REALLY, REALLY want him!"

Prayer: Lord, today I am thankful for the reminder of your presence, peace, protection, and provision. Guide me this day, to the honor and glory of your name. Amen.

Shazetta Thompson-Hill

Notes

FINDING VOICE

1. Marianne Schnall, "Madeleine Albright: An Exclusive Interview," Huffpost.com, June 15, 2010, www.huffpost.com/entry/madeleine-albright-an-exc_b_604418.

2. Teresa of Avila, *The Way of Perfection*, trans. E. Allison Peers (London: Sheed and Ward, 1999), 14.

3. As of 2019, there are thirty-six Doctors of the Church, of whom only four are women: Teresa of Avila, Catherine of Siena, Thérèse of Lisieux, and Hildegard of Bingen. See Mary T. Malone, *Four Women Doctors of the Church: Hildegard of Bingen, Catherine of Siena, Teresa of Ávila, Thérèse of Lisieux* (New York: Orbis, 2015).

4. James Martin, "Fr. James Martin on the Humor of St Teresa of Ávila," Order of Carmelites, October 14, 2013, www.carmelites.net/news/the-humor-of-st-teresa-of-avila/.

5. Ada Maria Isasi-Diaz, a mujerista theologian, used the term *kin-dom* instead of *kingdom* when referring to the reign of God in her work "Kin-dom of God: A Mujerista Proposal." This term takes away the hierarchical and especially patriarchal nature of word *kingdom* and uses a different term to emphasize the community and liberation.

6. Acts 17:28 NRSV

7. Brené Brown, *Braving the Wilderness* (New York: Random House, 2017), 40.

8. Mark 5:28

9. Rachel Held Evans, *A Year of Biblical Womanhood: How a Liberated Woman Found Herself Sitting on Her Roof, Covering Her Head, and Calling Her Husband "Master"* (Nashville: Thomas Nelson, 2012), 278.

10. Some passages in the Bible have been used as what is known as "clobber passages" to shame and condemn members of the LGBTQ+ community as it

relates to sexual orientation: "Don't you realize that the unholy will not inherit the kindom of God? Do not deceive yourselves: no fornicators, idolaters, adulterers, hustlers, pederasts, thieves, misers, drunkards, slanderers or extortionists will inherit God's kindom" (1 Corinthians 6:9-10 IB).

CULTIVATING PEACE

1. N. K. Jemisin, *The Killing Moon* (New York: Orbit, 2012), 335.

2. Nadia Bolz-Weber, *Shameless: A Sexual Reformation* (New York: Convergent, 2019), 19.

3. Fannie Lou Hamer, *The Speeches of Fannie Lou Hamer: To Tell It Like It Is*, ed. Maegan Parker Brooks and Davis W. Houck (Jackson: University Press of Mississippi, 2011), 136.

4. Catherine Marshall, *Christy* (New York: Avon Books, 1968), 44.

5. N. K. Jemisin, *How Long 'Til Black Future Month?* (New York: Orbit, 2018), 5.

6. Audre Lorde, "Chorus," *The Collected Poems of Audre Lorde* (New York: W. W. Norton & Company, 2017), 266.

FACING LOSS

1. "A Service of Death and Resurrection," *The United Methodist Book of Worship* (Nashville: The United Methodist Publishing House, 1992), 150.

2. Kerrie Hide, *Gifted Origins to Graced Fulfillment: The Soteriology of Julian of Norwich* (Collegeville, MN: Liturgical, 2001), 46.

3. Joyce Rupp, *Praying Our Goodbyes* (Notre Dame, IN: Ave Maria, 2009), 91.

4. I first spoke about my relationship with these verses around my pregnancy losses with the Rev. Tiffany Patterson, who wrote about my story in another book. There are echoes in this devotion from what I shared with her. See Brandy Mullins and Tiffany Patterson, *Out of the Depths: Your Companion After Pregnancy or Infant Loss* (Nashville: Abingdon Press, 2019), 30.

5. Elissa Schappell, "Toni Morrison, The Art of Fiction No. 134," *The Paris Review* (Fall 1993), www.theparisreview.org/interviews/1888/toni-morrison-the-art-of-fiction-no134-toni-morrison.

6. Emily Dickinson, "Ashes denote that fire was," *The Complete Poems of Emily*

Dickinson, ed. Thomas H. Johnson (New York: Little, Brown and Company, 1976), 1063.

Transforming Criticism

1. Michelle Obama, *Becoming* (New York: Penguin Random House, 2018), 25.

2. *The Book of Discipline of The United Methodist Church* (Nashville: The United Methodist Publishing House, 2016), ¶ 304.3.

3. Jan Richardson, *The Cure for Sorrow: A Book of Blessings for Times of Grief* (Orlando: Wanton Gospeller, 2016), 157–58.

4. This prayer references Psalm 139, Luke 23:34, and Romans 7:15-20.

Living Gratitude

1. Robin Stern and Robert Emmons, "Gratitude Practice Explained," Yale Center for Emotional Intelligence, November 23, 2015. http://ei.yale.edu /what-is-gratitude/.

2. Then God said, "Let us make humanity in our image to resemble us so that they may take charge of the fish of the sea, the birds in the sky, the livestock, all the earth, and all the crawling things on earth."

3. Barbara Grizzuti Harrison, "A Meditation on Eve," in *Out of the Garden: Women Writers on the Bible*, ed. Christina Büchmann and Celina Spiegel (New York: Ballantine, 1995), 1.

4. This prayer references Lamentations 3:22-23 (NRSV) and Galatians 5:22-23.

5. Although the Psalms were likely written by elite males—given the patriarchal structure of education, religion, and society at large at the time—women across the centuries have used and recited them, as evidenced in our Scriptures, and used them devotionally. This writer's decision to call this psalmist a woman, then, is a choice to reflect the importance of the Psalms throughout Judeo-Christian history in the lives of women.

6. Maya Angelou, *Letter to My Daughter* (New York: Random House, 2008), 459.

7. Barbara Brown Taylor, *An Altar in the World: A Geography of Faith* (New York: HarperOne, 2010), 117–18.

8. Rebecca O'Connell, "Cartoonist Shows Why You Should Say 'Thank You'

Instead of 'Sorry.' " *Mental Floss*, March 22, 2016. https://mentalfloss.com/article/77455/cartoonist-shows-why-you-should-say-thank-you-instead-sorry.

9. Tamora Pierce, *Trickster's Queen* (New York: Random House Children's Books, 2004), 302–3.

10. Psalm 121:4 (NRSV)

Contributors

The Rev. Quaya Rae Ackerman, MSM, Pastor, Arthur United Methodist Church (UMC), Arthur, ND

The Rev. Mara LeHew Bailey, Chaplain, Simpson College, Indianola, IA

The Rev. Amanda Baker, Pastor, Baldwin First UMC, Baldwin City, KS

The Rev. Jessica Lauer Baldyga, Associate Pastor, Centenary UMC, Effingham, IL

The Rev. Amelia Beasley, Pastor, El Mesías UMC, Mission, TX

The Rev. Lindsey Bell-Kerr, Pastor, Christ Church United Methodist and First United Methodist, Santa Rosa, CA

The Rev. Rachel Billups, Senior Pastor, Ginghamsburg Church, Tipp City, OH

The Rev. Katie J. P. Bishop, Senior Pastor, Greater Brunswick Charge, Brunswick, MD

The Rev. Katie Black, Associate Pastor, First UMC, Lake Charles, LA

The Rev. Michelle Bodle, Pastor, Philipsburg Grace/Morgan Run United Methodist Parish, Philipsburg, PA

The Rev. J. Paige Boyer, Campus Pastor, Simpson Metro West Campus of Westlake UMC, Cleveland, OH

The Rev. Jennifer Burns, Pastor, Memorial UMC, West Carrollton, OH

The Rev. Emily Spearman Cannon, Lead Pastor, McPherson First UMC, McPherson, KS

The Rev. **Laurel A. Capesius**, Director of Children and Family Ministries, La Cañada UMC, La Cañada, CA

Kai Carico, Director of Youth Ministries, First UMC, Oak Ridge, TN

The Rev. **Sarai Case**, Full Elder on family leave; Internal Communications Specialist for international, sustainability-focused corporation in Phoenix, AZ

The Rev. **April Casperson**, Director of Diversity and Inclusion, West Ohio Conference

The Rev. **Janessa Chastain**, Pastor, Grace UMC, Mesa, AZ

The Rev. **Catherine Christman**, Pastor, Stoughton UMC, Stoughton, WI

Lynnette Cole, Pastor, Schroon Lake Community Church, Schroon Lake, NY

The Rev. **Jessie Squires Colwell**, Lead Pastor, Rappahannock Charge UMC, Flint Hill, VA

The Rev. **Nicole Wiedman Cox**, Associate Pastor, Springfield First UMC, Springfield, IL

The Rev. **Paula Cripps-Vallejo**, Pastora, Iglesia Metodista Unida (Humboldt Park UMC), Chicago, IL

The Rev. **Andrea Curry**, Lead Pastor, Trinity UMC, Bowling Green, OH

The Rev. **Mary R. W. Dicken**, Pastor, Meridian Street UMC, Indianapolis, IN

The Rev. **Heather Dorr**, Pastor, Asbury UMC, Bettendorf, IA

The Rev. **Alexa Eisenbarth**, Pastor, Orting UMC, Orting, WA

The Rev. **Melissa Engel**, Community Educator, Safe Journeys, Streator, IL

Kelley Fox, Development Assistant and Faith Organizer, Equality Ohio, Columbus, OH

The Rev. Lauren A. Godwin, Pastor, Grace UMC, Keyser, WV

The Rev. Anna Guillozet, Senior Pastor, Linworth UMC, Columbus, OH

The Rev. Sarah Harrison-McQueen, Senior Pastor, Central UMC, Arlington, VA

The Rev. Molly Simpson Hayes, Lead Pastor, Church of the Good Shepherd United Methodist, Arlington, TX

The Rev. Brooke Heerwald Steiner, Lead Pastor, Excelsior UMC, Excelsior, MN

The Rev. Karen Hernandez, District Superintendent, Sage District, Oregon-Idaho Conference of The UMC

The Rev. Brandi Tevebaugh Horton, Senior Associate, First Methodist Houston, Houston, TX

The Rev. Jill Moffett Howard, Senior Pastor, Rosedale Hills UMC, Indianapolis, IN

The Rev. Hyewon Sophia Hyon, Associate Pastor, First UMC, Chicago Temple, Chicago, IL

The Rev. Jodie Ihfe, Senior Pastor, First UMC, Johnson City, TN

The Rev. Breanna Illéné, Pastor, Trinity UMC; Content Curation and Ecumenical Innovation Coordinator, Wisconsin Council of Churches

The Rev. Crystal Jacobson, Pastor, Tanner Valley UMC, Lawrenceburg, IN

The Rev. Ashley Fitzpatrick Jenkins, Pastor, Senoia UMC, Senoia, GA

The Rev. Violet Johnicker, Pastor, Brooke Road UMC, Rockford, IL

The Rev. Nicole de Castrique Jones, Pastor, Morning Star UMC, Canton, NC

The Rev. Catherine Jordan-Latham, Pastor, Simply Grace UMC, Bloomsbury, NJ

The Rev. Sarah Karber, Campus Director of Spiritual Care, Augustana Health Care Center, Minneapolis, MN

The Rev. Diane M. Kenaston, Pastor, University UMC, St. Louis, MO

Kendall Kridner-Protzmann, Pastor of Congregational Care, St. Andrew UMC, Highlands Ranch, CO

The Rev. Rebecca L. Laird, Sr. Engagement Manager, University of Rochester Medical Center

The Rev. Katie Lloyd, Senior Pastor, Buechel UMC, Louisville, KY

The Rev. Kate Mackereth Fulton, Associate Pastor, St. Paul's UMC, Kensington, MD

The Rev. Gabrielle Marie Martone, Associate Pastor, Central UMC, Linwood, NJ

The Rev. Courtney McHill, Berlin, Germany

The Rev. Sara McManus, Pastor, Flame of Faith UMC, West Fargo, ND

The Rev. Jennifer Zeigler Medley, Chaplain, Ascension Sacred Heart Pensacola, Pensacola, FL

The Rev. Brandee Jasmine Mimitzraiem, Pastor, Quinn Chapel African Methodist Episcopal Church, Lincoln, NE

Mrs. Caroline Anne Morrison, Religious Affairs Specialist, Kansas Army National Guard

The Rev. Sara M. Nelson, Senior Pastor, First UMC, Watertown, SD

The Rev. Bich Thy (Betty) Nguyen, Congregational Resources Minister, Mile High Metro District, Denver, CO

The Rev. Cassandra Núñez, Associate Pastor, Bering Memorial UMC, Houston, TX

The Rev. Laura C. Patterson, Pastor, Eliam UMC, Elberton, GA

The Rev. **Katrina Paxson**, Minister, Beulah UMC, Valley, AL

The Rev. **Dr. Emily A. Peck-McClain**, Visiting Professor of Christian Formation and Young Adult Ministry, Wesley Theological Seminary, Washington, DC

The Rev. **Jessica Petersen**, Pastor to Children and Families, Bethany UMC, Austin, TX

The Rev. **Colleen Hallagan Preuninger**, Associate Minister, Memorial Church, and Director of Student Engagement, Stanford University, Stanford, CA

The Rev. **Lorrin M. Radzik**, Pastor, Rockport UMC, Rocky River, OH

The Rev. **Jessica Anne Richard**, Associate Pastor, Platte Woods UMC, Platte Woods, MO

The Rev. **Shannon Rodenberg**, Pastor, Fairland First UMC, Fairland, OK

The Rev. **Amanda M. Rohrs**, Pastor, Hurdtown UMC and The UMC of Lake Hopatcong, Lake Hopatcong, NJ

The Rev. **Stephanie Rupert**, Pastor, McVeytown and Wayne (Pennsylvania) United Methodist Churches

The Rev. **Elizabeth Ingram Schindler**, Lead Pastor, Faith UMC, Issaquah, WA

The Rev. **Allie Scott**, Pastor, Peace UMC, Brookfield, WI

The Rev. **Caitlin Simpson**, Pastor, New Life in Christ Christian Church (Disciples of Christ), Louisville, KY

The Rev. **Julia Singleton**, Pastor, Christ UMC, Brookhaven, PA

The Rev. **Kate E. Smith**, Pastor of Mission and Outreach, Hyde Park Community UMC, Cincinnati, OH

The Rev. **Nancy Speas**, Freelance Writer and Editor, Nashville, TN

The Rev. **Debbie Sperry**, Pastor, Moscow First UMC, Moscow, ID

The Rev. **Katharine L. Steele**, Chaplain Resident, Kettering Health Network, Grandview Medical Center, Dayton, OH

The Rev. **Emily L. Stirewalt**, La Monte and Eldorado (Missouri) United Methodist Churches

The Rev. **Megan Stowe**, District Superintendent of the Central Massachusetts District, New England Conference, Methuen, MA

The Rev. **Shannon E. Sullivan**, Associate Pastor, Calvary UMC, Frederick, MD

The Rev. **Hillary Taylor**, Pastor, Bethany-Zoar United Methodist Charge, Saluda, SC

The Rev. Dr. **Theresa S. Thames**, Associate Dean of Religious Life and the Chapel at Princeton University, Princeton, NJ

The Rev. Dr. **Shazetta Thompson-Hill**, Associate Pastor, Christian Chapel Temple of Faith (Christian Methodist Episcopal), Dallas, TX

The Rev. **Shannon V. Trenton**, Pastor, Church of the Redeemer UMC, Cleveland Heights, OH

The Rev. **Corey Tarreto Turnpenny**, Pastor, Whitney Point UMC, Whitney Point, NY

The Rev. **Jen Tyler**, Pastor, Evergreen UMC, Wahpeton, ND

The Rev. **Alison VanBuskirk Philip**, Pastor, Franklin Lakes UMC, Franklin Lakes, NJ

The Rev. **Kate Walker**, Pastor, Deer Park UMC, Deer Park, TX

The Rev. **Bethany Willers**, Pastor, The United Methodist Church and The Methodist Church in Britain

The Rev. **Arionne Yvette Williams**, Associate Chaplain, University of Indianapolis, IN

The Rev. **Blair Boyd Zant**, Associate Director, North Georgia UMC Center for Congregational Excellence, Atlanta, GA